Table of Contents

The Psychologist-Manager Journal
Vol. 3, Number 2

Psychology Press
Taylor & Francis Group

New York   London

The Psychologist-Manager Journal

An Official Publication of the Society of Psychologists in Management

Editor

Rodney L. Lowman
California School of Professional Psychology

Editorial Board

Contributing/Consulting Editors

Kenneth Ball, Ken Ball Management Resources
Linda S. Gottfredson, The University of Delaware
Ann Howard, DDI
Charles Kiesler, San Diego, California
Richard Kilburg, John Hopkins University
Harry Levinson, The Levinson Institute
Paul Lloyd, Southeast Missouri State University
Robert P. Lowman, The University of North Carolina – Chapel Hill
Edward J. Pavur, Jr., Assessment and Development Management Service
Hendrick W. Ruck, US Air Force

Production Editors

Steve Crabtree, The Gallup Organization
Robin MacKnight, The Gallup Organization

Section I:

MANAGEMENT PRINCIPLES: THE THEORY OF MANAGEMENT

The Psychologist-Manager Journal
1999, Vol. 3, No. 2, 125-141

The History of Organization Development and the NTL Institute: What We Have Learned, Forgotten, and Rewritten[1]

Arthur M. Freedman[2]

Quantuum Associates

This paper traces the origins and history of the National Training Laboratories (NTL), and addresses the influence of NTL on the development of the field of Organization Development (OD). Historical and environmental factors are discussed in the context of the NTL's evolution. The article provides a case study of the managerial issues involved in operating a not-for-profit, value-laden, member-based professional association.

Organization development (OD) is a discipline or a craft—but it is not yet, I believe, a profession. Yet, OD theory, strategies, and methodologies have exerted considerable influence in shaping other disciplines, including the practice of management. Understanding some of the history of OD—the description of which is the purpose of this article—may be an essential contextual addition to OD's practical conceptual framework, strategies, methodologies, and philosophical values. The history of the field of OD cannot be separated from that of the NTL Institute for Applied Behavioral Science. Similarly, the history of NTL cannot be separated from that of the refugee German-Jewish psychologist, Kurt Lewin.

The timelines presented in this article (See Figures 1-7) are intended to reflect some of the important events in the history of OD. As can be seen from these diagrams, the timelines (directional arrows) run from left to right through the middle of each page. Above the directional arrows, relevant global and national events are identified. In this article, I have tried to depict some of the external events and forces that have influenced the evolution of NTL and OD, and to describe some of the products and services that were generated. Below the directional arrows I have described some of the events that occurred within NTL and among the Institute's members during the same decade.

History of NTL and Organization Development

The 1930s

External events and forces. In the mid-1930s, the United States was in the depths of the Great Depression. Frederick Taylor's "scientific management" (Taylor, 1911/1967) was the dominant model at that time for organizational consulting. Organizational structure was still traditional and somewhat authoritarian, although companies like DuPont and General Motors had developed the divisional form of corporate governance. The implications of The Hawthorne Studies were still being teased out of the writings of Mayo (1933) and Roethlisberger and

Figure 1
The History of Organization Development & NTL: 1930-1939

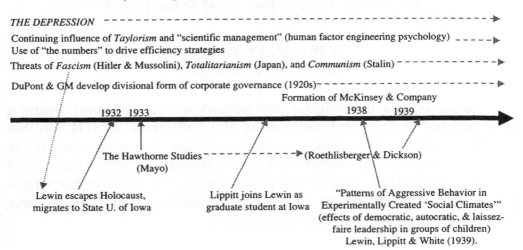

Dickson (1949). Much of the rest of the world was just beginning to allow itself to become aware of the triple threat to democracy and capitalism: Hitler's and Mussolini's fascism, Japan's semi-divine totalitarianism, and Stalin's communism.

Fleeing from Nazi Germany, Kurt Lewin, one of the early pioneers of OD, obtained refuge at the State University of Iowa (Marrow, 1969). Much of his family—most notably, his mother—did not survive the holocaust. Lewin fell in love with America. He fully believed that democracy was both the antidote for and inoculation against political and social oppression. At about this time, he also began experimenting with Action Research. In the mid-1930s, Ron Lippitt became one of Lewin's graduate students. Lewin, Lippitt & White (1939) published the results of their famous studies of auto-cratic, democratic and laissez-faire leadership styles. Then the Second World War began.

The 1940s

External events and forces. The 1940s was a decade of intense, varied, and rapid developments all over the world. The most significant events were, of course, the Second World War and the Holocaust. Almost incidentally, Norwegian freedom fighters developed self-organizing teams. After WWII, American soldiers returned, only to discover a paucity of housing and jobs. The GI Bill of Rights (Marrow, 1969) helped by enabling a large number of veterans to obtain college educations. However, in spite of the then-recent experiences with fascism and total-itarianism, there was a considerable amount of bigotry, discrimination, and prejudice within American society. Some people claimed this was a predictable function of too many people competing for too few, finite resources. Saul Alinsky published *Reveille for Radicals* (Alinsky, 1946) in which he described values, strategies, and methods through which communities could organize themselves to deal with their social issues in ways that enhanced their members' autonomy, self-determination, and self-esteem. Alinsky's work added to and philosophi-cally supported the community development work of Ronald Lippitt

Figure 2
The History of Organization Development & NTL: 1940-1949

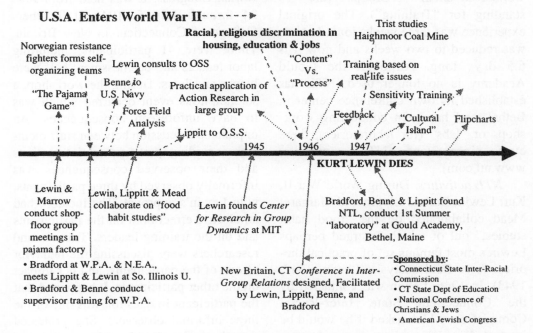

(1949). Alinsky and Lippitt influenced many NTL members who were intensely involved in such social action projects as the War on Poverty in the 1960s. Their theories and methods were eventually incorporated into those of OD.

Internal Developments. When WWII ended, the full extent of the Holocaust was revealed in horrific detail. Lewin was convinced that the democratization of America and its institutions was the only viable means of preventing a recurrence. He and his family moved to Newtonville, near Boston, to found the Center for Research on Group Dynamics at the Massachusetts Institute of Technology. Simultaneously, he launched the Commission on Community Interrelations in New York for the American Jewish Congress (Marrow, 1969).

In the early 1940s, Lewin and Eric Trist had met several times to discuss the implications of the Haighmoor Coal Mine Study for planned organizational change.

Each would later say that these discussions were mutually stimulating and that each learned something useful from the other's experiences. Alfred Marrow wrote that he had dropped in on Lewin one evening after the Connecticut Conference (see below) and found him hard at work, and exhausted. Marrow was alarmed by what he saw and suggested that Lewin was working too hard. His response to this well-meaning advice was that his mother had died in Auschwitz, and that he therefore had no time to relax. Lewin died of a heart attack on February 11, 1947 (Marrow, 1969).

By the summer of 1947, Lee Bradford, Ronald Lippitt, and Kenneth Benne had founded the NTL Institute as a non-profit educational institute. The first summer workshop was conducted at the Gould Academy in Bethel, Maine, consistent with Lewin's belief that intense personal learning experiences should be conducted in a "cultural island." They called the process that was at the core of these workshops "Sensitivity Training." They worked in small "T-Groups" (the "T" standing for "Training"). The original experience was three weeks long. Later it was reduced to two weeks and now it is 6.5 days long. Although the Gould Academy is no longer used, NTL has established its own conference center in Bethel, and has been conducting workshops or "labs" (for laboratories), there ever since (see NTL's website, www.ntl.com).

NTL activities. During World War II, Kurt Lewin, Ronald Lippitt and Margaret Mead collaborated on the "food habit studies," out of which emerged perhaps Lewin's most famous set of practical theories: force field analysis (Lewin, 1942, 1943). In 1946, Lewin was contacted by the Connecticut State Inter-Racial Commission, which asked if he would be interested in designing and presenting a seminar/workshop in community leadership. Participants would walk away with practical skills to enable them to help black and Jewish Americans deal with three manifestations of discrimination, in housing, education, and jobs. Lewin had been developing some large group "experiments" that seemed quite relevant for this request. He enlisted Lippitt, Benne and Leland Bradford as co-trainers. Morton Deutsch, Murray Horwitz, Arnold Meier and Melvin Seeman served as observer-researchers during the workshop. Apparently, Dorwin Cartwright, Rensis Likert, Douglas McGregor, Alfred J. Marrow, Leon Festinger, Charles Myers, Henry Murray, Gordon Allport and J. R. P. French, among others, served as secondary researchers for the project.

"The Connecticut Conference" was co-sponsored by the Connecticut State Inter-Religious Commission, the Connecticut State Department of Education, the National Conference of Christians and Jews, and the American Jewish Congress. It was held from June 24 through July 6, 1946 at Teachers College of Connecticut in New Britain. There were 41 participants, including labor leaders and businessmen; half were blacks and Jews. During the workshop, a serendipitous event occurred which was to have unforeseen consequences. An unplanned discussion between staff members regarding participants' interactions and their observed consequences was informally observed by three participants, with Lewin's approval. The incident had an electric effect both on the participants and on the training leaders. Trainers and researchers were discussing the behavior of one of the participants, and her impact on the other participants. It happened that the participant in question was one of the three informal observers. She protested that she had not said or done what was being reported. The other two participants and the trainers and researchers assured her that she had, in fact, acted in that fashion. The other two participants added how they thought and felt about her behavior. She took in that information and, in subsequent meetings, demonstrated that she could modify her behavior based on that input. The trainers and researchers were stunned. They defined the interactions and called it "feedback."

Before many evenings had passed, all participants, the commuters as well as the residents, were attending these sessions. Participants reported that they were deriving important understandings of their own behavior and of the behavior of their groups. To the training staff it seemed that a potentially powerful medium and process of re-education had somewhat inadvertently been identified. If they were more or less objectively confronted with data concerning their own behavior and its effects, and if they participated nondefensively in thinking about implications of these data, participants achieved highly meaningful learnings about themselves, about the responses of others to them, and about group behavior and group development in general. They discovered the beneficial impacts of interpersonal feedback.

The significance of the entire experience was multi-dimensional. This new approach was a practical application of action research in a large group context. The implications of the distinction between "content" and "process" were clarified. The conference focused on training based on real-life issues. The beneficial consequences of interpersonal feedback were noted, studied, and clarified. Those of us who studied Lewin's original design noted the many points of similarity with what are now known as "future searches" (Weisbord, 1993) and "appreciative inquiry" (Cooperrider, 1986; Cooperrider & Srivastva, 1987).

The purposes of the conference and of the participants have often been distorted. For example, one author, Art Kleiner (1996), stated that the purpose had been to create "better ethnic relations, particularly between blacks and Jews [emphasis added]." I clearly remember Kenneth Benne and Ronald Lippitt telling me—separately and on different occasions—that both blacks and Jews were working together to deal with a common social problem that impacted both groups equally: discrimination in education, housing, and jobs. Perhaps relations between the populations did improve as a consequence, but that would have been a side-effect.

After Lewin's untimely death, Ronald Lippitt and the Center for Research in Group Dynamics moved to Ann Arbor and the University of Michigan. NTL

overcame its shaky beginnings and grew. One of NTL's core values was to give what was learned away to people who could use the knowledge. There was no sense of proprietary information, and copyrights were not used. Individuals studied a variety of topics and had their results typed up, duplicated and distributed widely. There were no names on the papers.

Lippitt told me about another manifestation of the "give it away" philosophy. It seems that the widespread practice of using flip-charts got its start at Bethel. Once Lippitt and Bradford stopped in the Bethel General Store on Main Street to pick up some meat for dinner. They were bemoaning the fact that the observer-researchers could not use chalkboards to capture at one time all of the process notes derived from a group discussion. Once the chalkboard was filled it had to be erased. They discussed their shared concern for lost information as the butcher pulled a large sheet of oiled paper—two feet wide and three feet long—from a thick roll that was anchored in a heavy iron paper holder screwed into the top of a table. Bradford and Lippitt continued their conversation, but their eyes were riveted to the butcher's process of wrapping the meat in the oiled paper, sealing it with masking tape and weighing the package. It was as if the butcher was performing an arcane religious ritual; the two of them watched intently while he used a grease pencil to write the price of the purchase on the top of the package.

They asked the butcher to sell them some of the butcher paper. They then had one of the custodians at Bethel build a wooden tripod. The next morning, Bradford and Lippitt displayed the world's first flip-chart. Finding that butcher paper was expensive, they went to the town's only newspaper and asked if they could

Figure 3
The History of Organization Development & NTL: 1950-1959

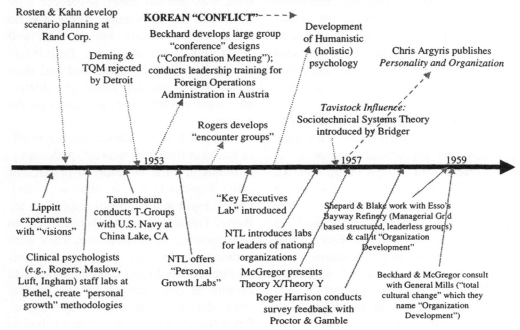

buy the end runs of the large rolls of newsprint. To this day, NTL has a tradition of buying those "end runs." In 1949, Lippitt published *Training in Community Relations*, a major contribution to the field of community organization and development. So, contemporary participants are often confused when NTL old-timers talk about "butcher paper" or "newsprint" instead of "flip-chart" paper.

The 1950s

The "Korean conflict" began to heat up in the early 1950s. W. Edwards Deming and his radical Total Quality Management (TQM) approach was rejected by Detroit auto manufacturers. He shifted his focus to Japan, with General Douglas MacArthur as his sponsor. In 1957, Harold Bridger brought his version of Sociotechnical Systems Theory to Bethel from the Tavistock Institute in England. E. Wight Bakke (1959) published the first formal evalua-

tion of executive education and training in participative management.

In the early 1950s, Lippitt began to experiment with "visions" of future states. Shortly after these experiments began, Leo Rosten and Herman Kahn developed scenario planning at Rand Corp. In 1952, Robert Tannenbaum began to export T-Groups from the cultural island at Bethel and applied the method with U.S. Navy personnel at China Lake, California.

In the late 1950s, Richard Beckhard developed and later published two extremely effective large-group "conference" designs for use within organizations: The Fact-Finding Conference (Schmidt & Beckhard, 1962) and The Confrontation Meeting (Beckhard, 1967). He also began to conduct experiential leadership training programs for the U.S. Foreign Operations Administration in Austria. Joseph Luft and Harry Ingham created the elegantly simple, yet profound, "Johari Window" in the late 1950s

(Luft, 1963, 1969). They, along with a number of other clinicians, began to offer "personal growth" labs through NTL.

Around 1955, NTL began to offer "Key Executives Labs." In 1956 it began to offer labs for leaders of national organizations and associations. It was about this time that the clinicians who had been coming to NTL since the beginning of the decade developed a sub-practice area within the psychological profession called humanistic (or holistic) psychology. In the late 1950s, Douglas McGregor (1960) began to formulate and present his Theory X and Theory Y for the first time. Chris Argyris began his prolific series of publications (1957), which persistently emphasized that organizational effectiveness was a function of the members' (behavioral) interpersonal and group competence. In 1958, Roger Harrison conducted survey feedback (heavily influenced by Rensis Likert and Floyd Mann) with Proctor & Gamble. Dorothy Stock and Herbert Thelen (1958) researched group dynamics in T-Group settings and applied many of the results to therapy groups. These tentative efforts to apply what had been learned in Bethel to real-life organizations culminated in two critical experiences in 1959. First, Herbert Shepard and Robert Blake worked with Esso's Bayway Refinery using the Managerial Grid™ and structured, leaderless T-Groups. They called this unique effort "Organization Development." At the same time, Richard Beckhard and Douglas McGregor were consulting with General Mills on a "total cultural change." They also named their rather distinctive effort, "Organization Development." These efforts developed independently. So the simultaneous naming of the field by independent parties seems to have been coincidental.

The 1960s

External events and forces. In 1960, Lyndon Johnson orchestrated the passage of legislation requiring mandatory retirement at age 65. This led to the realization that many top managers in major corporations would retire within two years, with few qualified replacements. This situation created significant business opportunities in leadership training and development, not only for NTL but for most management consulting firms as well. In 1963, after the Rochester riots, Saul Alinsky demonstrated the power of his community organization strategies and tactics by targeting Eastman Kodak to reverse its alleged irresponsible and discriminatory policies and practices toward some employees and the communities in which their plants were located (Alinsky, 1971-1972).

The period from 1964 to 1965 was marked by what was probably the most significant series of events of the 20th century. These started with Dr. Martin Luther King, Jr.'s activities that led to groundbreaking civil rights legislation, and the "War on Poverty."

Emery and Thorsrud (1976) introduced the radical concept of "industrial democracy" in the United Kingdom and Western Europe. In 1968, Alinsky engineered the shareholders' protests at Eastman Kodak, in an effort to hold the corporation accountable for its acts of commission and omission regarding its previously undifferentiated masses of investors.

Internal developments. Judging by the steady increase in participation at the Bethel labs in the early and mid-1960s, this was probably the "Golden Age"—or decade—for NTL, although we did not realize it at the time. In late 1961, Shepard and Davis and brought Tannenbaum, Beckhard and Ferguson, into TRW to help senior Personnel staff acquire skills

Figure 4
The History of Organization Development & NTL: 1960-1969

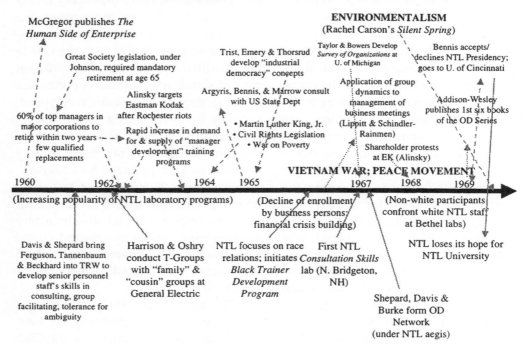

in consulting, group facilitation, and tolerating ambiguity.

In 1962, Harrison and Oshry conducted T-Groups with "family" and "cousin" groups at General Electric. This was based on the reasonable assumption that since T-Groups worked so well with "stranger" groups at the Bethel cultural island, they should be even more effective with people who worked closely together on a day-to-day basis. This assumption proved to be totally unrealistic.

Carl Rogers (1965) participated in at least one NTL lab in Bethel, applying T-Group theory and methods to group psychotherapy and coining the term, "Encounter Groups." Abraham Maslow also spent some time in Bethel in the early 1960s, and later (1965) published personal notes on his observations of the operations of a highly effective electronic plant. These demonstrated the extent to which he was influenced by the demo-

cratic, participative group and intergroup processes in which he had participated while at NTL labs.

In 1965, Argyris, Marrow, and Warren Bennis began to consult with the U.S. State Department. Marrow (1974) published an interesting little book about this failed consultation. Mark Chesler and Robert Fox (1966) published a book on role-playing that contributed to the andragogical educational methodologies that have been typical in NTL's training programs.

Rensis Likert (1961) and Floyd Mann (1957) influenced James C. Taylor and David G. Bowers (1967) who developed the Survey of Organizations (SOO) at the University of Michigan. This was the first "machine-scored, standardized" employee survey instrument, and it enabled the development of survey-guided OD interventions (Nadler, 1977). In 1967, NTL designed and presented its first workshop on Consultation Skills in North Bridgeton, NH. Shepard, Davis, and W. Warner Burke formed the OD Network (ODN), under the aegis of NTL. In 1969, Addison-Wesley published a boxed set of the first six books in its new series on OD (Beckhard, 1969; Bennis, 1969; Blake & Mouton, 1969; Lawrence & Lorsch, 1969; Schein, 1969; Walton, 1969). This was a landmark event, as a major publisher acknowledged, and, to a great extent, legitimized the fledgling OD discipline by initiating a continuing series of books about various aspects of the field.

The year 1966 was the beginning of a moral, ethical, and financial crisis within NTL. Driven by the civil rights, anti-Vietnam, and peace movements, NTL moved to correct the apparent "racial imbalance" in NTL's membership. NTL initiated the "Black Trainers Development Program." Schindler-Rainmen and Lippitt (1970-72) applied group dynamics to the management of business meetings focusing on policy-making, problem-solving, and decision-making. In the summer of 1969, non-white participants in NTL programs at Bethel confronted white NTL staff about what they claimed to be the Institute's "institutionalized racism and sexism" in 1968.

Around 1969, Warren Bennis accepted the invitation to succeed Bradford as President of NTL, but only after the Board of Directors agreed to take on considerable debt to buy an option for land to comply with Bennis' wishes to build the NTL University. However, it is said that Bennis left NTL after he received and accepted an invitation to become the president of SUNY-Buffalo. NTL thus lost its best hope for the future, and incurred a huge debt that would take most of the next decade to pay off (verbal history and Bennis, 1994).

The 1970s

External events and forces. Early in the 1970s, Affirmative Action legislation created a new market for NTL. This development added to NTL's concerns about racial and gender issues that had emerged in Bethel in the summers of 1968 and 1969. The legislation also opened the doors to a vast opportunity— or so it seemed at the time.

The 1971 global oil crisis had many consequences, including the ascendance of Japanese auto manufacturers. This, among other factors, led to a re-evaluation of American manufacturers' prevailing assumptions and business strategies. It led to an appreciation of "competitive advantage" and a new openness to TQM as a means of competing with Japan. The oil crisis also precipitated a paradigm shift to more global perspectives. By 1977, Reductions-In-Force (RIFs) had become a popular corporate tactic for reducing costs. Of course, this led to an enormous number of dislocated or displaced workers and managers.

In 1972, University Associates capitalized on NTL's inattention to its proprietary interests and published the first of its Annual Handbooks (Pfeiffer & Jones, 1972) which, initially, consisted almost entirely of anonymous, non-voluntary "contributions" by NTL members.

Internal developments. In 1970, Malcolm Knowles published a very influential book that differentiated between androgogy and pedagogy. Knowles was a professor at the School of Education at Boston University who was impressed by the experiential methods used in "human relations training" and frequently discussed issues of adult education with Benne and the rest of us at the Human Relations Center.

In 1974, Chris Argyris and Donald Schön developed and published their concept of "theories in action," which they

Figure 5
The History of Organization Development & NTL: 1970-1979

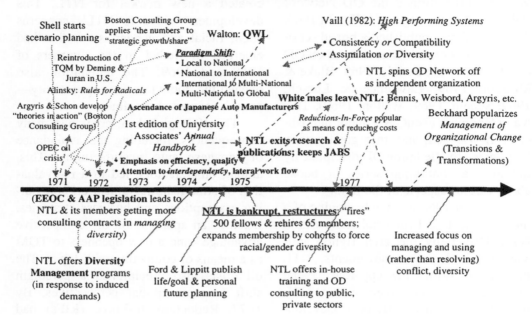

derived from work with a major Boston-based consulting firm. A year later, Dick Walton (1972) began to popularize the concept of "Quality of Work Life" at NTL's labs (Skrovan, 1983). While this issue was very compatible with NTL's values, and was actively endorsed by most of our members, it was not well accepted by the Institute's profit-oriented clientele. Lippitt began to popularize his process for enabling individuals to imagine and plan how to create compelling and meaningful futures for themselves (Ford & Lippitt, 1988).

Most significantly, NTL decided to exit its very influential publishing business. This abandonment of NTL's pre-eminent position as the leading organization in the field of OD was as mysterious as it was paradoxical. OD practitioners were just beginning to successfully sell their services to a skeptical market. The field was beginning to attract a dramatic increase in numbers of self-proclaimed and semi-trained consultants. Affiliation

organizations like the Organization Development Network (ODN) had thousands of members; the OD Institute (ODI) was in a rapid start-up mode. Articles by and about OD began to appear in such journals as *Harvard Business Review, Sloan Management Review, Training & Development Journal, Administrative Science Quarterly,* and *Personnel.* This was also about the time when organizations like TRW, Digital Equipment, and G. D. Searle were building up their staffs of internal OD consultants. Publishers like University Associates, Addison-Wesley, and Jossey-Bass took over the OD publishing business.

In 1977, NTL began to seriously market in-house training and OD and diversity consultation to public and private-sector organizations. This created some conflict because it put NTL in competition with its own members. Perhaps to cut costs, NTL spun off the ODN as an independent membership organization.

In 1978 and 1979, Beckhard continued to popularize the management of organizational change through his NTL-based "Change Management Workshops," entrepreneurial workshops, articles and books. Diluted versions of his work have since become extremely prominent in the services offered by the Big-5 management consulting firms, in relation to their business process reengineering and information technology-driven organizational change practices. NTL increased its conceptual focus to market the concepts of conflict management and utilization (rather than conflict resolution) and continued its emphasis on diversity management.

During the 1970s, a number of universities—for example, George Williams College, Benedictine College, Pepperdine University, Fielding Institute, and the Union Graduate School—began master's degree programs in OD and human resource management. A few doctoral programs also emerged, most notably that of Case-Western Reserve University and, more recently, Benedictine University. Today, there are over 20 universities in the US alone that offer graduate degrees in OD. But until the '70s, most advanced degrees in OD-related topics were identified as "Organizational Behavior." Hybrid programs in which OD was the primary focus did exist—for example, the Ed.D. and certificate programs offered at Teachers College at Columbia University by former NTL members (e.g., Burke and Hornstein). NTL chose not to affiliate itself with most of these university-based programs until 1979, when it partnered with American University in developing the American University/NTL Master's Degree specializing in Human Resource Development. Later, this was changed to an MSOD degree.

Internal developments. In the early 1970s, NTL began to shift its philosophy away from democratization toward "social justice." This added to the growing philosophical schism between members who believed in objective third-party consulting with total systems, and those who believed that it was a moral imperative to advocate diversity issues that were of particular concern to "disenfranchised" constituencies. Non-white and female NTL members also derived benefits from this focus: training and consulting contracts that were initiated through participants with whom they established contact at NTL labs.

NTL chose to ignore developments taking place in its market environment—particularly the so-called Quality Revolution. The Institute increased its focus on diversity management while continuing to market its programs to business and industry.

In essence, the inauguration of University Associates' Annual Handbooks in 1972 had an adverse impact on two of NTL's early "businesses" by publishing the results of its empirical action research into interpersonal, group, intergroup, organizational and community dynamics and OD consulting. NTL chose to largely exit the research and publishing businesses—though it did continue to publish *The Journal of Applied Behavioral Science* and an occasional book, like the *Consultation Skills Reading Book* (Lee & Freedman, 1984), *Reading Book for Human Relations Training* (Porter & Mohr, 1982), and *Managing in the Age of Change* (Ritvo, Litwin & Butler, 1995).

In 1975, NTL almost went bankrupt and was forced to radically restructure itself. All of its 500 Fellows, Members, and Associates were "fired." About 75 were "rehired." Around this time, NTL lost a lot of its creative talent either because they were excluded from re-entry to the organization, or because for various

Figure 6
The History of Organization Development & NTL: 1980-1989

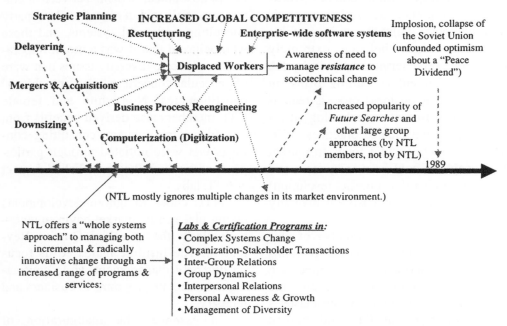

reasons they declined the invitation to re-enter. For example, Warren Bennis, Marvin Weisbord, Chris Argyris, Harvey Hornstein, Warren Burke, and Barry Oshry were NTL members before 1975 but were no longer members after 1976.

By 1977, NTL no longer held a leadership position in the field of OD. Its primary organizational effort focused on avoiding extinction. In addition, "professional" NTL members who had been serving as business managers at the central office were replaced by naive but enthusiastic professional administrative staff. NTL's focus became one of maximizing revenues and reducing costs; ensuring program quality or customer service became secondary issues. Many participants were accepted into advanced labs without having participated in prerequisite labs. The size of the T-Groups was allowed to increase beyond the traditional 12-person limit. In the late 1970s, intraorganizational political schisms that

reflected ideological differences contributed to NTL's becoming increasingly marginalized and irrelevant—at least as far as the continuing development of the field of OD was concerned.

The 1980s

External events and forces. The implosion and collapse of the Soviet Union from 1989 through 1991 signaled major international changes and a movement further away from autocratic systems of governing. This suggested the unprecedented validation of the resilience, endurance and power of democracy and a free market economy. In the increasingly competitive, global, deregulated market environment, organizations sought competitive advantages through strategic planning, de-layering, mergers and acquisitions, downsizing, business process reengineering, outsourcing, restructuring, computerization of production and information management systems. The implicit psychological contract between employees and employers was broken by massive layoffs. The management consulting divisions of the large accounting firms, and an incredible number and range of small, medium, and large consulting firms, grew and gradually began to replace the freelance consultant. They "borrowed" and re-labeled psychological and OD theory for their marketing, which proved to be quite successful, if not effective.

Internal developments. The major activity at NTL during this decade was the repackaging of workshops into certificate programs in diversity management, OD consultation, laboratory-based or experiential education, and the like.

This was a decade during which ideology truly replaced action research within NTL. What could have been a remarkable opportunity for NTL to re-establish itself was ignored or neglected. The 1980s and 1990s had been decades of radical, unprecedented and discontinuous change in the national, regional, and global environments, but NTL did not address these changes with any sustained vigor. A few NTL workshops, such as "Consultation Skills" and "Facilitating and Managing Complex Systems Change," remained relevant. Peter Vaill (1982) began to publish his ideas about "high-performing systems," which might have been exploited as the basis for a series of public programs and consultative services.

The 1990s

External events and forces. Throughout the 1990s, world leaders became increasingly aware of multiple threats, on a global scale, posed by forces that promote social, geopolitical, and economic turmoil. These destabilizing forces include nationalism, ethnic and tribal conflicts, and terrorism, and the proliferation of democracies and free market economies in developing countries around the globe.

Particularly since the mid-1990s, organizational leaders and their internal staff groups also seem to have become aware of—and to accept—the idea that their organizations' cultures and traditional management practices can either enable or obstruct the effective application of strategic, structural, procedural, or technological innovations to their businesses. Further, they have become aware that unmanaged "culture clashes" can sink a merger or acquisition.

Internal developments. Although it has been taught and written about for years, process facilitation became popular in the early 1990s through Edgar Schein's publications and Brendon Reddy and Chuck Phillips' NTL publications and workshops. Jim Collins and Jerry Porras (1998) published a meaningful and scholarly alternative to Peters and Waterman's inspirational best-seller, *In Search of Excellence* (1982). Again, Collins and Porras' work could have been—but was not—used as the basis for a new generation of relevant NTL workshops and consultative services.

During the early 1990s, NTL was faced with an identity crisis that continues today: is the Institute to continue to evolve into a moralistic, anti-oppression advocate for its own aggressive version of social justice? Or is NTL an Institute that conducts research in the applied behavioral sciences, then publishes and uses the results to create and deliver experiential, andragogical training programs that provide participants with the concepts, strategies, methods, and personal skills needed to enhance democratic processes? Can it be both? Further, is NTL to be an Institute with a regional, national, or global scope?

Figure 7
The History of Organization Development & NTL: 1990-1999

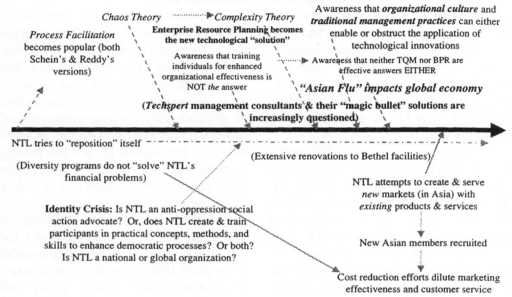

INCREASED RECOGNITION OF MULTIPLE THREATS, ON GLOBAL SCALE, OF NATIONALISM, ETHNICITY, RELIGION, & "TRIBALISM"

NTL's recurrent financial crises triggered a great deal of consternation among the Board of Directors, its leadership, membership and administrative staff. The possibility of bankruptcy has been very real. The selected recovery strategy has focused almost exclusively on cost-cutting, augmented by appeals for donations of time and money from members, and their estates. NTL's central office staff has been reduced. Marketing and customer service functions have been under-funded as a result.

Conclusions

There are many managerial implications embedded in this review of NTL's distinguished—and often anguished—past. As I consider the developments of NTL's last three decades, I see a disturbing bifurcation. For many reasons, including financial exigencies, NTL seems to have abandoned its pre-eminent position and moved to the less influential fringes of OD. Functional leadership in the OD field has been assumed by various associations, universities, and consulting firms. For most younger or newer OD educators and practitioners, NTL seems to be perceived as a quaint anachronism that has some historical significance. Painfully for me, many of these folks do not even recognize NTL's name.

Other centers of OD practice—the associations like ODN and ODI, the university programs, the small OD-oriented consulting firms, and even the infant change management practices that have been added by many management consulting firms—have taken a far more pragmatic, results-oriented approach, with less exclusive emphasis on diversity, self-awareness, and interpersonal and group skills.

NTL needs to confront and work through Peter Drucker's (1992) fundamental questions: what businesses should NTL be in?; what is its mission?; what does NTL, as an organization, do better than anyone else?; what are its competitive advantages? I argue that the answer is three-fold: a) the design and delivery of laboratory-based, andragogical or experiential education; b) the application of action research methods and values to real-life situations; and c) high-involvement, participatory planning and implementation. These happen to be three of the three primary elements of OD. As an organization, NTL does not have exclusive or unique competencies in the second or third areas. However, there are few, if any, real alternatives to NTL for the first competitive advantage. The challenge is: how can NTL, as a not-for-profit organization, leverage these competencies in a competitive environment in order to survive and flourish in the future?

References

Alinsky, S. (1946). *Revelle for radicals*. Chicago: University of Chicago.

Alinsky, S. (1971). *Rules for radicals*. New York: Random House.

Argyris, C. (1957). *Personality and organization*. New York: Harper & Row.

Argyris, C. (1960). *Understanding organizational behavior*. Homewood, IL: Dorsey Press.

Argyris, C. (1962). *Interpersonal competence and organizational effectiveness*. Homewood, IL: Irwin-Dorsey Press.

Argyris, C. (1965). *Organization and innovation*. Homewood, IL: Irwin-Dorsey Press.

Argyris, C., & Schon, D.A. (1974). *Theories in practice: Increasing professional effectiveness*. San Francisco: Jossey-Bass.

Bakke, E. W. (1959). *A Norwegian contribution to management development*. Bergen, Norway: The Administrative Research Foundation at the Norwegian School of Economics and Business Administration.

Beckhard, R. (1967/1969). The confrontation meeting. *Harvard Business Review. Human relations, Series II. Reprints from the Harvard Business Review* (pp. 133-139). Cambridge, MA: Harvard Business School Press.

Beckhard, R. (1969). *Organization development: strategies and models*. Reading, MA: Addison-Wesley.

Benne, K. D. History of the *T*-group in the laboratory setting. In L. P. Bradford, J. R.Gibb, & K. D. Benne (1964). *T-group theory and laboratory method*. New York: Wiley & Sons.

Bennis, W. G. (1969). *Organization development: Its nature, origins, and prospects*. Reading, MA: Addison-Wesley.

Bennis, W. (1994). *An invented life*. Reading, MA: Addison-Wesley.

Blake, R. R. & Mouton, J. S. (1969). *Building a dynamic corporation through grid organization development*. Reading, MA: Addison-Wesley.

Bradford, L. P. (1976). *Making meetings work: A guide for leaders and group members*. La Jolla, CA: University Associates.

Chesler, M. & Fox, R. (1966). *Role-playing methods in the classroom*. Chicago: Science Research Associates.

Collins, J. C. & Porras, J. I. (1998). *Built to last: Successful habits of visionary companies*. New York: Harper Business.

Cooperrider, D. (1986). *Appreciative inquiry: A methodology for understanding and enriching organizational innovation*. Ann Arbor: University Microfilms International.

Cooperrider, D. and Srivastva, S. (1987). Appreciative inquiry in organizational life. *Research in organizational change and development, 1,* 129-169.

Drucker, P. F. (1992). *Managing for the future: The 1990s and beyond.* New York: Truman Talley Books/Dutton.

Emery, F. & Thorsrud, E. (1976). *Democracy at Work. Studies in the Quality of Working Life: No. 2.* Norwell: Kluwer Academic Publishers.

Ford, G. & Lippitt, R. (1988). *Creating your future: A guide to personal goal setting.* San Diego: University Associates.

Jayaram, G. K. (1976). Open systems planning. In W. G. Bennis, K. D. Benne, R. Chin, & K. E. Corey (Eds.) *The planning of change* (3rd ed.). New York: Holt Rinehart & Winston.

Kleiner, A. (1996). *The age of heretics.* New York: Currency Doubleday.

Knowles, M. S. (1970). *The modern practice of adult education: Andragogy versus pedagogy.* New York: Association Press.

Lawrence, P. R. & Lorsch, J. W. (1969). *Developing organizations: Diagnosis and action.* Reading, MA: Addison-Wesley.

Lee, R. J. & Freedman, A. M. (Eds.) (1984). *Consultation skills readings.* Arlington, VA: NTL Institute.

Lewin, K. (1935). The conflict between Aristotelian and Galileian modes of thought in contemporary psychology. *Journal of General Psychology, 5,* 141-177.

Lewin, K., Lippitt, R., & White, R. (1939). Patterns of aggressive behavior in experimentally created "social climates." *Journal of Social Psychology, 10,* 271-299.

Lewin, K. (1942). *The relative effectiveness of a lecture method and a method of group decision for changing food habits.* Washington, DC: Committee on Food Habits, National Research Council.

Lewin, K. (1943). Forces behind food habits and methods of change. *National Research Council Bulletin, 108,* 35-65.

Likert, R. L. (1961). *New patterns of management.* New York: McGraw-Hill.

Lippitt, R. (1949). *Training in community relations.* New York: Harper & Bros.

Luft, J. (1984). *Group processes: An introduction to group dynamics* (3rd ed.). Mountain View, CA: Mayfield Publishing.

Luft, J. (1969). *Of human interaction.* Palo Alto, CA: National Press Books.

Lynton, R. P. & Pareek, U. (1967). *Training for development.* Homewood, IL: Irwin-Dorsey Press.

Mann, F. C. (1957). Studying and creating change: A means to understanding social organization. *Research in Industrial Social Relations, 17,* 146-167.

Marrow, A. J. (1967). Events leading to the establishment of the national training laboratories. *Journal of Applied Behavioral Science, 3.*

Marrow, A. J. (1969). *The practical theorist: The life and work of Kurt Lewin.* New York: Basic Books.

Marrow, A. J. (1971). Events leading to the establishment of the national training laboratories. *Journal of Applied Behavioral Science, Kurt Lewin Commemorative Issue.* New Britain, CT: Human Resource Center for Consultation.

Marrow, A. J. (1974). *Making waves in Foggy Bottom.* Washington: NTL Institute.

Maslow, A. H. (1965). *Eupsychian management: A journal.* Homewood, IL: Irwin-Dorsey Press.

Mayo, E. (1933). *The human problems of*

an industrial civilization. New York: Macmillan.

McGregor, D. (1960). *The human side of enterprise.* New York: McGraw-Hill.

Nadler, D. A. (1977). *Feedback and organization development: Using data-based methods.* Reading, MA: Addison-Wesley.

Peters, T. J. & Waterman, R. H. (1982). *In search of excellence: Lessons from America's best-run companies.* New York: Harper & Row.

Pfeiffer, J. W. & Jones, J. E. (1972). *The 1972 annual handbook for group facilitators.* Iowa City, IO: University Associates.

Porter, L. & Mohr, B. (Eds.). (1982). *Reading book for human relations training.* Alexandria, VA: NTL Institute.

Ritvo, R. A., Litwin, A. H. & Butler, L. (Eds.). (1995). *Managing in the age of change: Essential skills to manage today's diverse workforce.* Burr Ridge, IL: Irwin Professional Publishing.

Roethlisberger, F. J. & Dickson, W.J. (1949). *Management and the worker.* Cambridge, MA: Harvard University Press.

Rogers, C. R. Dealing with psychological tensions. *Journal of Applied Behavioral Science, 1*, 6-24.

Schein, E. H. (1969). *Process consultation: Its role in organization development.* Reading, MA: Addison-Wesley.

Schindler-Rainman, E. & Lippitt, R. (1970-72). *Team training for community change: Concepts, goals, strategies and skills.* Riverside, CA: University of California Extension.

Schmidt, W. H. & Beckhard, R. (1962). The fact-finding conference. In W. W. Burke, & R. Beckhard (Eds.), *Conference planning, Selected reading. Series Six* (pp 68-73). Washington, DC: NTL and NEA.

Skrovan, D. J. (Ed.). (1983). *Quality of work life.* Reading, MA: Addison-Wesley.

Stock, D. & Thelen, H. (1958). *Emotional dynamics and group culture.* New York: New York University Press.

Taylor, F. W. (1911/1967). *The principles of scientific management.* New York: W. W. Norton.

Vaill, P. B. (1982). The purposing of high-performing systems. *Organizational Dynamics,* Autumn, pp. 23-39.

Walton, R. E. (1969). *Interpersonal peacemaking: Confrontations and third-party consultation.* Reading, MA: Addison-Wesley.

Walton, R. E. (1972). How to counter alienation in the plant. *Harvard Business Review, 50,* 70-81.

Weisbord, M. R. (1993). *Discovering common ground: How future search conferences bring people together to achieve breakthrough innovations, empowerment, shared vision, and collaborative action.* San Francisco: Berrett-Koehler.

---

[1]Portions of this article were presented as the author's Presidential Address, delivered at the annual meeting of the Society of Psychologists in Management, Tampa, FL, 1999., Tampa, FL.

[2]*Correspondence to:*
Arthur M. Freedman, Ph.D.
Quantuum Associates
1000 Lake Shore Plaza, Suite 24C
Chicago, IL 60611
E-mail: arthurf796@aol.com

SOCIETY OF PSYCHOLOGISTS IN MANAGEMENT

The Society of Psychologists in Management (SPIM)
is a unique organization of psychologists dedicated to the growth and development of its members, who work as leaders or managers or who focus on applying psychology to management.

SPIM invites new members who share our common interests. Consider the benefits of SPIM membership if you are a psychologist who . . .

- holds a position of leadership in your organization
- works as an executive or manager
- conducts psychological research on management
- consults with executives or managers on psychological issues
- has started your own business or consulting practice

Benefits of SPIM membership include . . .

- an opportunity to network with some of the most innovative psychologist-managers in the country.
- an outstanding annual winter conference with continuing education credit recognized by the American Psychological Association.
- *The Psychologist Manager Journal,* sent to all SPIM members at no additional charge. The *Journal* contains elements of a scientific forum and a professional guide to good managerial practice.
- *The SPIMLetter,* a newsletter for all SPIM members published four times per year.

Membership materials can be obtained from:

Ms. Lorraine Rieff
SPIM Membership Administrator
1716 W. Touhy
Park Ridge, IL 60068
phone: 847/518-8277 ◆ fax: 847/518-8218 ◆ e-mail: lrieff@naii.org

Or download a SPIM membership form from the SPIM website at
http://www.spim.org

Section II:

LIVE FROM THE FIRING LINE: THE PRACTICE OF MANAGEMENT

The Psychologist-Manager Journal
1999, Vol. 3, No. 2, 145-146

Duke Ellington: Profile of a Leader

Douglas W. Bray[1]

DDI

This paper considers the ways in which Duke Ellington, whose birth centennial was celebrated in 1999, was a leader. The article contrasts some of the common assumptions about characteristics of a good organization (e.g., assumptions of egalitarianism and cordial relationships with peers) with the realities of how Duke Ellington managed his world-famous band. Ellington achieved excellence through selection, elitism, sharing the credit, personal role modeling, and incorporating his musicians into his creations. The results included very high levels of allegiance and creative talent.

This year, 1999, marks the centennial anniversary of the birth of Edward Kennedy "Duke" Ellington, the genius who created and performed his unique music for more than four decades. Born in Washington on April 29, 1899, Ellington came to New York in the early 1920s (Hasse, 1995; Yanow, 1999). By 1927, his band was ensconced in Harlem's legendary Cotton Club, from which network radio broadcasts three nights a week paved the way for coast-to-coast tours by "Duke Ellington and his Famous Orchestra." Ellington not only created a new music constructed, as a centennial article in the *New Yorker* (Balliett, 1999) noted, of undreamed of instrumental harmonies, but his productivity was astounding. His compositions numbered in the thousands. It is said that he wrote music in the hospital up to the day of his death.

But Duke Ellington was not only remarkable as a composer. He was a leader who kept his orchestra together for many years. The duration of its members' service was legendary, commonly 25 years or more. Baritone saxophonist Harry Carney, whom Duke recruited when he was 17, was with Ellington for 47 years up, until Duke's death.

Organizational psychologists may well wonder how such permanence of personnel was achieved. The life of a band member was not easy. Long national tours were made via the band bus. Concerts were often one-night stands, and overnight travel was all too common. The musicians sometimes played two cities in a row, sleeping in the bus. Their travels kept them away from their families and friends for long periods. International travel added to these separations.

Ellington did not achieve the long-term allegiance of his men through personal intimacy. A striking example is the fact that the Duke did not travel with his musicians on the band bus. Instead, the aforementioned Harry Carney, who loved to drive, chauffeured Ellington all over the country in a luxury sedan. Nor did Ellington bother himself with relationships among the band members. He kept a strictly hands-off attitude, expecting them to settle their own problems as adults. And problems there were! Some of the men were not on speaking terms with others, and fisticuffs were not unheard of.

What did keep the band together for so long? In addition to steady and good pay, the members of the band enjoyed worldwide travel, playing in many nations for audiences which frequently included celebrities, sometimes even heads of state. They shared in the irresistible charisma of their leader. As trumpeter Clark Terry put it, it was like being on the New York Yankees. They had a dedicated role model. Duke lived to create and perform music. He would often stay at the piano long after the band had left, developing a new creation, and he vexed Broadway impresarios by hitting the road instead of preparing for a show he was to do with them in New York. After all, he could keep in touch from Omaha or Laramie without depriving audiences in the hinterland of his music.

The stability of the band, once described as Ellington's musical instrument, was essential to Duke's creativity. Unlike composers who write scores to be played by various orchestras, Ellington composed for his particular musicians. He knew each of their unique sounds and styles, and his compositions were tailored to them, whether they were to play a long solo, play a few solo measures, or simply to accompany others. He valued and respected them as unique contributors. A trombonist once joined the band and set about trying to duplicate the solos of a great Ellington trombonist who had absented himself for a time. Duke told the recruit not to do this, saying, "I want you to sound like you!" Ellington always shared the applause, introducing soloists, for example, as "Our All-American baritone saxophonist" or "a trumpeter beyond category."

So the members of the band had an incomparable role model. But the great regard held by Duke's musicians was due to the idea that his music was their music. Their parts in the never-ending stream of compositions, many of which would be played for years to come, were ideally suited to their unique instrumental voices and styles. And they knew that their voices and styles had reverberated in Duke's imagination as he composed the classics they would play. He wrote for them and they played for him. Who would want to leave?

References

Balliett, W. (1999, February 1). Mood Ellington. *New Yorker* p. 85.

Hasse, J.E. (1995). Beyond category : *The life and genius of Duke Ellington.* New York: DaCapo Press.

Yanow, S. (1999). *Duke Ellington.* New York: Friedman/Fairax.

---

[1]An earlier version of this paper was presented at the annual meeting of the Society of Psychologists in Management, Tampa, February, 1999.

Correspondence to:
Doug Bray, Ph.D.
DDI
21 Knoll Rd.
Tenafly, NJ 07670

The Psychologist-Manager Journal
1999, Vol. 3, No. 2, 147-148

Introduction to Special Section on Technology and Its Impact on the Psychologist-Manager

Albert R. Hollenbeck[1]

AARP Research Group

In this introduction to a special section of *The Psychologist-Manager Journal* on "Technology and Its Impact on the Psychologist-Manager" (Hollenbeck, 1999), the general themes of the special section are identified, along with the increasing role that technology necessarily plays in the life of the psychologist-manager.

This special section is derived from a series of presentations made at the 1999 Mid-Winter Conference of the Society of Psychologists in Management in Tampa on the theme, "Looking to a Hard and Soft Future: Technology and its Impact on the Psychologist-Manager." The presentations provided an overview of the potential of technological advances for psychologist-managers.

Technological changes are occurring so rapidly that those of us who work daily with technology sometimes feel as if it is a hopeless task to stay abreast of change, let alone to find the time to optimally apply current technology to business problems facing our organizations. The purpose of this collection of articles is to extend knowledge of the most effective uses of technology in management by the psychologist-manager. A common theme of these articles is the application of principles we as psychologists follow in order to assist our organizations, businesses and clients as they struggle with the range of technological issues affecting employees and customers.

Each article covers different aspects of the applications of technology to management. Civiello (1999) discusses the role of the psychologist-manager in dealing with organizational threats from cyberspace. Hollenbeck (1999) identifies everyday Internet tools useful to the psychologist-manager, and outlines a program of Internet research initiated at a large non-profit organization. Greenberg (1999) provides an overview of the use of technology for traditional psychological assessments in the workplace. Cryer and Hollenbeck (1999) describe the development of techniques for making group decisions in a business setting using electronic group-decision tools. The final article expands and deepens the discussion of technology use for the psychologist-manager by providing an empirical study of emerging technologies and their impact in a work setting (Habash, 1999). Finally, Reaser (1999) and Conklin (1999) provide commentary on the articles in the series and add their own perspectives on technological issues for the psychologist-manager.

Psychologist-managers are just beginning to explore and write about the technologies discussed in this special section. Most psychologist-managers seem to have become involved with these technologies for a pragmatic reason—we had to learn them as skills needed for use in our jobs. Now, our jobs have often become technology-intensive—both in the research of technologies and in their application to specific management tasks. Articles such as those in this special section can assist us in these times of rapid technological change. They can help us address the larger human issues that arise with any major change—and technology is certainly that—in the workplace.

References

Civiello, C.L. (1999). Cyberspace, trusted insiders, and organizational threat: The role of the Psychologist-Manager. *The Psychologist-Manager Journal, 3,* 149-166.

Conklin, J. (1999). Technology and organizations: Internet impacts on managers and management. *The Psychologist-Manager Journal, 3,* 191-197.

Cryer, R. and Hollenbeck, A.R. (1999). Case study: Traditional facilitation skills combined with group decision technologies. *The Psychologist-Manager Journal, 3,* 191-195.

Greenberg, C.I. (1999). Innovations and advancements in technology for psychologists working in organizations. *The Psychologist-Manager Journal, 3,* 167-176.

Habash, T.C. (1999). The impact of audio- or video-conferencing and group decision tools on group perception and satisfaction in distributed meetings. *The Psychologist-Manager Journal, 3,* 205-224.

Hollenbeck, A.R. (1999). Introduction to the special section on technology and its impact on the psychologist-manager. *The Psychologist-Manager Journal, 3,* 147-148.

Hollenbeck, A.R. (1999). Using the Internet and World Wide Web (WWW): Amazing sites/amazing insights. *The Psychologist-Manager Journal, 3,* 177-189.

Reaser, J.M. (1999). New technologies and old issues: Musings of a cyber-pioneer. *The Psychologist-Manager Journal, 3,* 199-202.

[1]*Correspondence to:*
Albert R. Hollenbeck, Ph.D.
AARP
601 East St, NW
Washington, DC 20049
E-mail: ahollenbeck@aarp.org

The Psychologist-Manager Journal
1999, Vol. 3, No. 2, 149-166

Cyberspace, Trusted Insiders, and Organizational Threat

Cathleen L. Civiello[1, 2]

U.S. Government, Owings Mills, Maryland

This article examines managerial roles in identifying and influencing computer-based activity that poses risks to an organization's activities, facilities and personnel, and securing methods for addressing the behavioral sequelae associated with cyberthreat. The article argues that addressing external threats and technical aspects of internal threats is best left to information security professionals. Psychologist-managers, however, are in a unique position to address the risks posed by trusted insiders and former insiders affiliated with their organizations through assessment and intervention. Strategies to facilitate the assessment of such risk, as well as countermeasure strategies, are proposed.

The use of computers, the availability of technological applications, and access to the Internet, both in organizational and home environments, are all expanding exponentially (O'Shea, 1999). Unfortunately the behaviors of users are not all positive, and some may threaten the viability, or even the very existence, of an organization. Organizational vulnerability is also rapidly increasing, particularly as related to the impact of computer misuse and computer-related criminal behavior committed by trusted insiders. This article reviews the phenomena of cyberthreat and discusses some roles psychologist-managers can play in understanding and influencing the behavior and its sequelae.

Computer Crime

Specific areas in which computer crime may manifest itself as a risk to organizations were summarized well by Harris (1995). The use of computers in crime is presented as an overriding risk factor. Three components of cyberspace criminal activity were identified (Harris, 1995): the computer as a criminal tool, the computer as a target of criminal activity, and the computer used in an incidental manner as part of a criminal offense. It is important to consider these three areas in the context of computer misuse by trusted insiders within organizations in order to understand the potential negative organizational influences. This paper will explore risk factors, and factors that mitigate risk, posed by trusted insiders when they misuse an organization's computers, regardless of whether or not the intent at the time of the misuse was criminal. Trusted insiders—primarily, but not exclusively, employees of an organization—are those with authorized access to an organization's information systems. Examples of non-employee trusted insiders include contract professionals who maintain an organization's information systems, and customers who use those systems.

Of the components discussed by

Harris (1995), computer use incidental to criminal activity is probably of least interest to psychologist-managers. This component is, however, important when identifying partners in risk mitigation. Specifically, the computer, even when not specifically used in behavior that poses a risk to an organization, may contain information that is important to the identification, evaluation, and/or reduction of organizational threat.

When computers are targets of criminal activity or misuse, those who pose the risk are seldom trusted insiders. The exceptions are the disgruntled trusted insiders or former trusted insiders who intentionally sabotage an organization's information systems. There are many other reasons why a computer may be targeted, but unless it is for the purpose of sabotage, considering such behavior as a means to an end will facilitate the identification of both risk and risk mitigators.

In the majority of instances of computer misuse in an organization, the computer is a tool or a means to an end. Risk factors relating to such misuse can be generalized to sabotage risk factors in many cases, and will be the main focus of the remainder of this paper.

Economic/Industrial Espionage and Theft of Trade Secrets

Economic Espionage Act of 1996

Passage of the Economic Espionage Act (18 USCS Section 1831, Lexis, 1999) and the Theft of Trade Secrets Act (18 USCS Section 1832, Lexis, 1999) in 1996 promised to stem the ever-increasing tide of proprietary information theft. These laws established criminal and civil consequences for the theft or destruction of a trade secret with the intent to benefit a foreign power. Consequences were also applicable to those with the intent to ben-

efit anyone other than the owner, or with the intent to injure the owner, of a trade secret. Unfortunately, by 1997 the scope of the problem was increasing rather than decreasing. There were over 1,100 documented incidents and another 550 suspected incidents of economic espionage that year (Foreign Spies Increase Attacks, 1998). In addition, the dollar loss was five times greater than the annual loss estimated prior to passage of the two acts. Denning (1999) reported that estimated annual corporate losses are in excess of $250 billion, and further reported that over half of the *Fortune* 1000 and the 300 fastest-growing U.S. companies reported being victimized when surveyed by the American Society for Industrial Security. The survey further identified the single greatest threat to proprietary information or other organizational secrets as the trusted insider, closely followed by former trusted insiders.

Organizations increasingly need to worry about foreign governments from at least 28 countries, including U.S. allies, targeting them with the intent to steal trade secrets (Foreign Spies Increase Attacks, 1998). President Clinton, in his annual report to Congress on foreign economic collection and industrial espionage, confirmed this activity by stating that in 1997 there were at least 23 countries involved in such targeting, with the bulk of their activities focused on trade secrets (Starr, 1997). Although the methodology involved in stealing such secrets can include intrusive methods such as bugging offices or hacking into computer networks, direct contact with trusted insiders poses significant risks (Foreign Spies Increase Attacks, 1998).

Trade secrets are basically information, regardless of type or storage method, that provides or potentially provides value to an organization. To be classified as a trade secret, the information must not be readily discernible by the public. Another critical criterion included in the Economic Espionage Act requires that, for information to qualify as a trade secret, the company must have taken reasonable measures to protect that information. Such reasonable measures involve not only technological solutions provided by information security professionals, such as penetration tests, but also security precautions concerning those to whom the organization allows access to its critical information.

Scope of the Problem

Industry. The scope of the problem is broad and growing. The threat of specific economic espionage, as discussed above, is increasingly intertwined with cyberthreat issues. Pinkerton surveyed *Fortune* 1000 executives and determined that executives in service businesses considered hardware and software theft to be their top security threat (Pinkerton, 1999). Cyberspace appears to play a central role in the growth of this problem. The Internet is the fastest-growing method of economic spying today. It provides a clear source from which spies may gather U.S. trade secrets (McKenna, 1997). In fact, information loss and theft of trade secrets are three times more prevalent in organizations engaged in business on the Internet (Dalton, 1998).

Theft of trade secrets is not limited to currently trusted insiders. Managers increasingly need to protect their business processes from being compromised by departing employees. Although companies have always lost employees to competitors, the rapidity of technological advances dramatically increases the risk associated with loss of intellectual property (Hibbard, McGee, and Wilder, 1998). Theft of trade secrets appears to be the most significant and highly publicized corporate cyberthreat issue, but other behaviors also pose threats to organizations. Since they are not as well publicized, the scope of such problems is difficult to determine.

Health care. Traditionally, the focus of work in this area has involved protecting trade secrets, intellectual property, and companies' proprietary information. Concern about protecting organizational information should not be limited to these traditional areas. Any information that is valuable to an organization and which can be used or abused by others should be viewed as vulnerable to exploitation by both trusted insiders and by those who gain unauthorized access. This includes information in health care settings. Examples of cyberspace attacks in health care settings include a case in London in which test results were changed to indicate that a woman without cancer did have signs of cancer, a case in which an AIDS research laboratory in Italy lost 10 years of data in a hacker attack, and a case in which a software bug in the computer program of a heart monitor led to the death of at least one patient ("A Matter of Life and Death," 1999).

The Psychology of Cyberspace

I found no empirical research that specifically addressed the risk factors associated with trusted insiders who misuse organizational information systems. Nonetheless, managers cannot afford to wait to address this problem because of its scope and potential toll on the organization. In the interim, managers can obtain information from the limited literature on the psychology of technology, from traditional organizational threat assessment practices, and from the clinical understanding of individual and organizational dysfunctions offered by psychology, in order to understand and assess risk, and develop risk mitigation strategies.

Self-Psychology in Cyberspace

Cyberspace provides the user with the opportunity to explore different aspects of self—both self as the user perceives it to exist, and desired or postulated selves. It provides an unrestricted forum for experimentation with positive aspects of self, as well as the darker sides. This experimentation can lead to the shedding of inhibition and can potentially lead to damage to the self (Reid, 1998, and Turkle, 1995). In cyberspace, self-concept involves the self of the mind rather than the body (Preston, 1998). Taking this idea to the extreme, some have even hypothesized that people will eventually download their conception of self into the computer and live in the cyberworld without a physical body (Goertzel, 1998).

Relationship between computer and user. Growth of the information superhighway affects the growth of interpersonal communication, but communication in this medium is qualitatively different from traditional communication. Traditional transport of information, such as with print or video, degrades the information, forcing less information to be transmitted than in face-to-face (FTF) communication. The sheer size of cyberspace not only broadens the ability to transmit ideas, but as the quality of the sensory experience in cyberspace improves and approaches that of real life, the distinction between the idea and the transmitter of the idea blurs. The concept of feeling lost or adrift in cyberspace becomes a phenomenon similar to being lost in social situations, but without the reference point of live actors. Thus, the paradigm of communication is changing as the distinction between what was animate and what was inanimate fades in the cybermedium.

Sensory immersion into the computer is central to this paradigm shift. Visual displays in cyberspace allow spatial navigation with increasingly rich perceptual engagement (Preston 1998). Computer-generated stimuli can allow immersion to the degree that the perceptions of the user are submerged into computer-generated stimuli (Biocca and Delaney, 1995). Although such sensory immersion is typically discussed in context of "virtual reality," it should also be considered in the general context of cyberspace. The communication interface that facilitates such immersion is the interaction between the sensory channels of the user and aspects of cyberspace that include the actual physical media, the communication codes, and the information. The virtual world constructed using this interface exists only in the mind of the computer user, with the psychological threshold being the point at which the attention and perceptions are so immersed in the online stimuli that the user begins to feel some sense of "being there" (Biocca and Delaney, 1995). The degree of immersion appears to increase in inverse proportion to the age at which the user began to use the computer for communication. Risk appears to be related to the degree to which one can control one's communication, immersion, and suspension of belief. It impacts not only vulnerability to manipulation by others, but also one's ability to evaluate the validity of information, as well as one's vulnerability to computer misuse.

Dungeons and Dragons versus MUD characters. Multiple user dungeons, multi-user domains, or multiple user dimensions (MUDs) appear to be the cyberspace versions of the "Dungeons and Dragons" phenomenon of the 1970s and 1980s. The MUDs are a form of Internet chat. They are programs through which players, represented by a character or characters, interact in computer-stimulated environments. Unlike those in Dungeons and Dragons, the characters in the MUDs can be controlled either by a user or by a computer (Meyer, 1995). Because of the current bandwidth limitations of the Internet, these interactions are primarily text-based. They can include static graphic and/or pictorial representations of the self that exist in rooms created by members and described automatically when one enters the MUD (King and Moreggi, 1998).

Despite bandwidth limitations, computer games, simulations, and other cyber-contexts are becoming increasingly more realistic and engaging (Shapiro and McDonald, 1995). In MUDs, players often have several characters and may use the characters to experiment with different aspect of the self. As bandwidth expands and MUDs become more realistic, sensory immersion will likely increase even further, as will the potential for the identification of personal vulnerabilities from the experimentation with aspects of self. Exploitation of the personal vulnerabilities of others also becomes more likely.

"Star Trek" computers and holograms. The evolution of the interaction between the human (and alien) beings and the computer in the Star Trek television series and movies provides a useful analogy to the evolution of such relationships in real life. Although the computer had a voice in the first series, its function was that of a traditional computer: data storage, data retrieval, and simple data analysis. In the more recent series, the interactions have evolved to the point that computer-simulated "holodecks" can approximate places and times on earth with

which crew members can interact experientially. In addition, computer-simulated holograms have evolved from recorded greetings to approximations of sentient beings with whom the crew members interact as peers. Are such interactions so different from the interaction between humans and computer-controlled characters in MUDs?

Personalization of computers. People tend to anthropomorphize computers, developing attitudes, social orientations, and preferences toward them (Palmer, 1995). Different social content in computer displays leads to different responses from users (Preston, 1998). Such differences provide fertile ground for psychological interpretation and potential insight into the person that can be used to exploit the user. Although hard data about the psychological relevance of such information is not presently available, marketers regularly exploit information about Internet behavior and use it for targeted advertising. It is not unreasonable to conclude that others are using this information for more nefarious purposes.

Specifically, it is quite easy for anyone with the ability to access an organization's web site, physical plant location, and/or publications to identify the employees of any given organization. After identifying the employees, one can then use the Internet to accumulate vast amounts of personal data about them, including assets, driving records, military records, and employment history (Lane, 1997). Such personal background information further facilitates interpretation of and insights into one's personality and vulnerabilities.

Seduction: romantic and technical. As technological advances reshape forms of human communication, and as the growth of the Internet leads to an increasingly larger share of the population communicating via cyberspace both at work and at home, humans are increasingly coming to know one another and to form bonds using information media (Palmer, 1995). These cyber-relationships provide fertile ground for interpersonal exploitation. The risk is heightened by high levels of self-disclosure on the Internet (Joinson, 1998), coupled with a false perception of privacy while communicating in cyberspace—a feeling that is exacerbated by the fact that many cyberspace communications originate in the privacy of one's home.

The best reviews of research on communication in cyberspace are included in several of the chapters compiled by Biocca and Levy (1995a). Although communication and relationships occur with increasing frequency in cyberspace, the paradigm for discussing both communication and relationships is still that of face-to-face (FTF) interaction. FTF communication occurs across multiple channels and is rich with complexity, immediacy, and subtlety. Computer-mediated communication (CMC) has traditionally been considered interpersonally limiting and, as a result, a preferred media for task-oriented communication (Palmer 1995).

FTF communication provides the opportunity for validation of the communication of others by observing non-verbal cues that unintentionally leak and provide evidence of deception (Ekman, 1992). The apparent absence of such complex social cues in CMC can be viewed as limiting the nature of cyber-relationships (Shapiro and McDonald, 1995) and as leading to a reduction in the influence of social norms and constraints (Joinson, 1998). The development of virtual communities and virtual relationships suggests that the paradigm of FTF communication is not the only one that can lead to complex relationships, but the lack of social context cues may lead the user to project more of his or her own experiences, expectations, and subconscious interpretations on the communications of others, perhaps creating a sense of intimacy more quickly than in traditional FTF communication, in which there is multichannel feedback. This sense of intimacy may actually seem to be false.

However, it may not be false. The perception of privacy that occurs in cyberspace, along with the experimentation with various aspects of self and the absence of negative immediate feedback, provides a context in which it is more comfortable to say things that one would hesitate to share in FTF communication.

The methodologies used by perpetrators of commercial espionage include facilitating theft of information contained in documents or computer storage media, using the services of prostitutes to blackmail trusted insiders, and developing personal relationships with employees with access to trade secrets ("Foreign Spies Increase Attacks," 1998). The personal, intimate cyber-relationships and identification of vulnerabilities that can occur in cyberspace can greatly facilitate these methodologies.

Justification of Cyber-Betrayal

A variety of psychological techniques can be used by trusted insiders to justify betraying the trust of their organizations. The most frequent are those typically employed by disgruntled employees, but other justifications are even more suited to cyberspace.

Biocca and Levy (1995b) discussed the classic American belief that information, education and technology can be liberating and transforming. This belief, when combined with the traditional academic ethic that research and information are to be shared and used for the benefit of all, provides a rationalization for betraying an organization's trust by sharing sensitive information such as trade secrets or records.

More traditional criminal behavior has often been psychologically justified or rationalized, specifically by those claiming that white-collar crime is a second job, rather than a criminal activity, even while performing the crime against their employers while on the premises of their employers. Such rationalization will be even easier to apply to industrial espionage when cyberspace is used to commit the crime. Mintz (1999), for example, wrote of an employee who claimed as a defense that he was only moonlighting for the company to which he passed the trade secrets from his primary employer.

Internet Addiction: The Synergy of Cyberspace Addictions and Gambling Addictions

The debate continues over the existence of behavioral addictions such as addictions to gambling and sex. Grohol (1998) discussed the history of the similar debate over whether Internet addiction actually exists. His use of the term "online overuse" clearly identifies his position in the debate, in which he concludes that there is no convincing evidence for the existence of Internet addiction. Griffiths (1998) reviewed survey research on excessive Internet use and concluded that the data to date do not clearly confirm the presence of Internet addiction, but by using case studies and the traditional addiction diagnostic criteria, Griffiths was able to identify clear cases of addiction.

Gackenbach, Guthrie, and Karpen (1998) clarified a key aspect of the attraction of cyberspace when they discussed

the simple thrill of being connected and the emergence of the phrase "surfing the net." Specifically, they hypothesized that the feeling of being connected and the perceived ability to access virtually anything across space and time leads to this thrill. A parallel can be drawn between this thrill and the initial thrill or high that one experiences when ingesting certain substances. The question remains as to which aspects of online behavior are key to development of an addiction. This may be a central issue when looking at the misuse of cyberspace and its impact on organizations. Regardless, the key focus of psychologist-managers should be behavioral impact on the individual and the subsequent impact on the organization.

A core issue in the debate over the existence of Internet addiction is whether there can be a primary addiction to the Internet, or whether the Internet is a vehicle for other addictions, such as workaholism and addiction to pornography. Whatever the definition of the behavior, the reality of misuse of computers in the workplace represents a legitimate concern for psychologist-managers. Online time not spent on work-related activities interferes with job performance. Illegal online behavior, such as trading child pornography, is a problem wherever it occurs, but a definite problem when it occurs in the workplace and/or while using company resources. Misuse of company equipment and Internet accounts that may implicate the company or influence others regarding the reputation of the company or agency should also concern the psychologist-manager.

Cybersex

Reversal of the social norm "don't talk to strangers" is inherent in cyberspace communication (King and

Moreggi, 1998). This reversal leads to saying and confiding what one would not say or confide in FTF communication, particularly as related to one's sexuality. Noonan (1998) discussed anonymity in cyberspace as related to sexual activities in which aspects of the physical and/or social self are changed or omitted, which probably further contributes to communication ease in CMC.

Sexual behavior is prevalent on the Internet, and dissemination of sexual material began early in Internet history. The first alternative sex (alt.sex) newsgroup appeared on April 3, 1988 (Noonan, 1998) in response to the demand for recreational online sex. Sexual content mushroomed from that point. That trend may be reversing. It is estimated that about 10% of merchant sites on the Web involve adult entertainment, but that the percentage will decrease to about 4% over the next few years because of the increase in Internet use by women and the elderly (Noonan, 1998). This estimate does not include interpersonal exchanges involving sexual content. These interpersonal exchanges are prime areas for targeting of one's employees based on vulnerabilities identified in newsgroups. There is a newsgroup for just about every paraphilia, facilitating normalization of such behavior.

Cyberspace Threat Assessment: Factors to Consider

In assessing organizational threats from cyberspace, many of the factors are the same as those associated with traditional threat assessment and risk management, as performed by psychologists and other professionals. The challenge is to consider the unique context and methodologies associated with cyberspace.

Access to Company Secrets/ Medical Records

Who and what? Igbaria, Shayo, and Olfman (1998) discussed the manner in which global economics are driving expansion of the virtual workplace, as firms routinely move work products around the world over the Internet. As a result, the assessment of who has access to which secrets, records, and information is more difficult than ever, but is the first step in any threat assessment. The purpose of this step is to identify an organization's trusted insiders, most of whom pose no organizational threat. This step helps to identify the pool of employees and organizational affiliates who have legitimate access—and the information to which they legitimately have access—in order to narrow the range of potential threats.

With the expansion of the number of employees working at home, and the explosion of traveling workers communicating with their workplace using Internet accounts, the ability to pinpoint the location of access to key information is also critical. This factor is especially important when considering former trusted insiders who may have continued access.

Personal needs. Any number of personal needs can be met by misusing the computer. Understanding the personal needs of trusted insiders will allow managers to increase the likelihood that those insiders will find solutions to their personal needs or problems in a manner that poses no risk to the organization. The following are only a few examples of personal needs that may lead to personal crises and precipitate a betrayal of trust via misuse of the organization's information systems.

Financial. Personal financial needs are the first and most obvious threat. For example, nine former trusted insiders of the Aydin Corporation allegedly misappropriated company secrets with the intent of forming a competing company (Aydin, 1998). Other types of financial needs that can be addressed by misusing computers include changing company records associated with compensation and money owed to the organization.

Relationship issues. Relationships, whether based in real life or in cyberspace, also provide fertile ground for strife and threat. When real-life relationships involve co-workers, cyberspace presents the opportunity to look for information that historically one may have looked for elsewhere. For example, if a system administrator suspects his or her co-worker spouse of having an affair with another co-worker, it may be tempting to intercept e-mail correspondence between the two.

A great deal of work has been done exploring the issues of workplace violence and sexual harassment as related to relationships. Some issues in these categories are directly relevant to threats from cyberspace. The more tragic workplace homicide incidents come from examples that were the culmination of erotomanic stalking (Simon, 1996). Workplace cyberspace provides an additional medium for stalking behavior, particularly when the stalker has the capacity to e-mail or sleuth anonymously. Sexual harassment is another form of workplace violence that may contribute to a hostile work environment.

Internet Addiction?

Kimberly Young first presented the concept of Internet addiction at the APA convention in 1996. Her work is especially useful in the assessment of addictive online behavior and its impact on organizations. In her book *Caught in the Net,* Young (1998) discussed cases that involved people from all walks of life, and provided specific workplace examples. Young also discussed a survey of behavior that provided an estimate of the likelihood of addiction. Young's approach can easily be adapted as a tool for educating workers about inappropriate Internet behavior.

Internet addiction can influence behavior in the workplace in much the same manner as alcoholism and gambling addition and should be assessed and addressed in much the same way. The diagnostic criteria for pathological gambling (American Psychiatric Association, 1994) can easily be adapted and applied to cyberspace addiction by substituting "computer" and "Internet use" for the word "gambling" and substituting the word "time" for "money." Despite the controversy over whether Internet addiction is a disorder, the workplace influence of specific behaviors should be the focus of the assessment, not whether an actual addictive disorder is present.

An added complexity is that most workers today are more productive with the aid of a computer, and their jobs may involve Internet connectivity. As a result, treating Internet addiction is extremely complex and there are few specialists available. Even if the information system within an organization is not connected to the Internet, the potential exists for addiction on a limited network if there is the opportunity to develop cyber-relationships and/or to explore corporate files and web sites. Lowman (1993) provides a useful context for beginning to address this problem in his book on treating work dysfunctions. To effectively diagnose and treat addictive behavior as it occurs in the workplace, close coordination between a trusted insider's therapist and the workplace is critical. Such coordination will identify to the therapist the environments in which Internet addiction may manifest itself in the workplace, help the therapist understand the full range of potential workplace exposure to the object of addiction, and provide opportunities for the organization to develop workplace accommodation strategies.

Real Life or Cyberspace?

For many people, the distinction between the real world and the cyber-world can blur. Such a blurring plays a critical role in threats to the workplace. In fact, Gackenbach, Guthrie, and Karpen (1998) assert that one's perception of reality is a best guess and that maneuvering in cyberspace may create alternative realities. The level of sensory involvement appears to determine the extent to which the cyberworld is indistinguishable from the real world, and the extent to which the user will need to make increasingly sophisticated judgments about what is real and what is not (Shapiro and McDonald, 1995).

Distinguishing reality from unreality can be a challenging task for all, and in one sense is a marker of good mental health. Cyberspace complicates this because it allows for the easy creation of alternative realities. The ability to create those alternative realities may enhance an organization's strength (e.g., by facilitating the development of new products), but only if the person doing the creating maintains an appropriate balance between what is real and what is created. There are downside risks both to the individual's mental health and to his or her vulnerability as a target of cyber-criminals.

The psychologist-manager can play a pivotal role in these situations. If an organization's affiliate works and/or plays in cyberspace, determining the ability of the affiliate to distinguish between what is real and what is not real in cyberspace is

as critical as determining the ability to make such distinctions in real life. At work, such a distinction is critical in determining the effectiveness of the affiliate. In private, an inability to make the distinction increases one's vulnerability to targeting by cyber-criminals. The psychologist-manager can assist human resource professionals and other organizational managers by developing strategies to assess the ability of an affiliate or potential affiliate to make these distinctions. Such strategies can range from adapting in-box exercises so that they include tasks involving appropriate cyberspace reality discriminations, to developing simple structured interview strategies that address cyber-behavior within organizational settings.

Shapiro and McDonald (1995) discussed critical factors for determining what is real and what is not. The most important factor is the ability of the user to make internal checks of reality. Checking external facts helps also, but not as much as internal reality checks. According to these authors, three issues complicate the ability to judge whether or not something is real. The first is a bias toward believing things are both real and true. A second difficulty is that the historically effective ways to make reality judgments were based on degree of interaction. Real events typically require some degree of interaction. Traditional entertainment involved little interaction beyond passive attention. Cyberspace entertainment, however, increasingly demands interaction as a participant.

A third complicating factor is related to signal strength. Signal detection theory asserts that the stronger the signal strength, the more likely it is that the user will decide something is real. However, judgment influences such decisions. Increasing signal strength will allow for increases in sensory richness, which is likely the perceptual cue that leads to a judgment of reality (Shapiro and McDonald, 1995). This suggests that it is critical to assess the degree to which a user makes appropriate reality judgments when in strong sensory environments— which certainly describes many interactive computing situations.

Hackers: Thrill-Seeking or Criminal Behavior?

Many view hacking into corporate resources, particularly those related to the critical infrastructure of the US, as the bailiwick of foreign operatives, terrorists, and/or recreational hackers. Retired U.S. Air Force General Robert Marsh, head of the President's Commission on Critical Infrastructure Protection, estimated that about 80% of such unauthorized intrusions were by trusted insiders and not external hackers. He further stated that the bulk of such intrusions were a function of employee disgruntlement (Nordwall, 1997). In addition to attempted penetrations by disgruntled affiliates, the manager also needs to be concerned about trusted insiders who attempt penetrations in response to boredom or an interest in hacking, or just for the challenge.

Regardless of whether one talks about hackers, crackers, phreakers or the cyberpunk subculture (Balsamo, 1995; Hafner and Markoff, 1991; Levy, 1984), issues of cyberspace generational identity are critical to threat assessment. Key issues regarding this emerging culture include a resistance to organizational control, and the belief that technological access to information is a natural condition (Balsamo, 1995). The likelihood of attempted unauthorized access is greater among trusted insiders who hold such beliefs.

The result is users who are more comfortable with computers than with television, print media, and even FTF human relationships. Of greatest concern to organizations are those typically called "crackers," who perpetrate illegal breaking and entering schemes (Balsamo, 1995). Although illegal behavior would give most organizations pause, the basic hacker ethic is itself a corporate threat. For example, Balsamo (1995) identified the hacker ethic as the following: "(a) access to computers should be unlimited and total... (b) information should be free... (c) hackers should mistrust authority and promote decentralization" (p. 355). Some human resource professionals, in their efforts to fill critical technical positions, hire hackers and crackers because of their technical skills, ignoring the associated risks.

Once hackers are employed, risk issues can multiply within the organization. Cyberpunks use computers to spread the culture and create virtual communities. They perceive that they will be able to change the system from the inside (Balsamo, 1995). Employment of these types of individuals has important implications for corporate culture and threats to the organization. Understanding these threats gives psychologist-managers a unique perspective on the cultural expectations of their organizations, and on forces for cultural change.

Other subculture issues are also relevant, but should not be confused with threats. One example is that video gaming and computer programming are not merely leisure activities for Generation X, but rather are the media through which this generation encounters the world (Turkle, 1984). In addition, cultural change in cyberspace is a process of self-organization leading to a dramatic change of culture and consciousness (Goertzel,

1998). It is critical that managers understand computer subcultures if they are to evaluate and reduce threats to their organizations. A critical factor in defining such threats is understanding whether the norms of the subculture to which a particular insider or applicant subscribes are lawful, and whether they are consistent with respect for the rights and privacy of others. It also critical to understand the degree to which the affiliate obeys the norms of her or his culture, as that is a likely predictor of whether the individual will observe organizational norms. If the norms of his or her subculture are unlawful, the affiliate's dedication to those norms will be of concern.

Hackers, hobbyists, users, and abusers. Turkle (1995) makes a distinction between hackers and hobbyists. Whereas hackers engage in illegal boundary violations, Internet hobbyists not only respect legal requirements, they also respect the privacy of others. In order to assess their skills in computer security, hobbyists may create legal tests such as obtaining permission to attempt to violate the cyber-boundaries of a colleague's information system. Hobbyists do not feel entitled to view personal records simply because another user failed to disable the permission setting allowing such entry. A distinction between users and abusers is also useful when evaluating threats to the company. A trusted insider who is a user and/or a hobbyist is likely to pose significantly less threat than one who is a hacker and/or abuser. Cyberspace narcissism is another variable that may be critical in this differentiation. Violating boundaries simply to prove that it can be done is an abusive risk behavior.

Moral flexibility. The willingness of trusted insiders to put the organization's needs and others' needs, both at work and in their private life, above their own is a critical issue in any assessment of threat. Such an assessment is no less important when assessing cyberspace risk. The difference is that in cyberspace there are additional areas in which such behavior can manifest itself. Assessment of the level of inhibition and ego boundaries of the affiliate may be a factor in limiting exploitative behavior in cyberspace. "Flaming" (the act of sending an electronic posting or news message intended to insult, provoke, or rebuke) is a subset of disinhibited behavior, but not the only kind of disinhibition (Joinson, 1998). Assessing one's willingness to flame others and the presence or lack of insight into the effect of such behavior on the target of the flame may provide key data for risk assessment.

Other Criminal Behavior

The targeting of trusted insiders based on Internet behavior by those intending to harm the organization is a critical vulnerability that must be included in a thorough threat assessment. The Web site Dejanews (www.dejanews.com) allows any Internet user to view profiles of users who post to newsgroups (Reid, 1998). In addition to the ability of others to identify vulnerabilities based on Internet behavior, the information from Dejanews provides the identities of likely contacts for those intent on recruiting insiders to betray organizational trust.

Goertzel (1998) described his vision of how a "World Wide Brain" might emerge from existing hardware and software, especially knowledge management systems. The resulting infrastructure may facilitate exchanges of non-proprietary information for increased mutual intelligence. In light of the issues regarding exchange of proprietary information and emerging economic espionage discussed above, in addition to the value of expanding the free exchange of knowledge from academia to cyber-subcultures, it seems likely that this medium will become the economic espionage medium of the future.

A relevant example would be the case in which a researcher who is young enough never to have known life without computers as a communication tool has moved from working in academia to employment in a corporate research and development environment. When working in academia, the researcher had probably been freely exchanging research ideas with other academic colleagues throughout the world. That exchange, and the tools that combined the information from all parties, led to a qualitative improvement in either the information itself or the utility of the information. When the researcher moved to an environment in which it is important to protect even a preliminary idea, the researcher would have difficulty not using the powerful knowledge management tool that was previously so effective.

The Psychology of Cyberspace

Creating a Clear Corporate Policy

A clear corporate policy will become the key factor in risk mitigation for current organizational affiliates. The policy should clearly spell out which forms of cyberspace behavior are acceptable and which are not. The policy should also state that violations of the policy will be investigated and appropriate administrative action will be taken, including potential employment termination. It should also be clearly stated that law enforcement will be notified when appropriate.

The similarities between other forms of unacceptable workplace behavior (such as violence) and those forms occurring in cyberspace may lead an organization to use an existing workplace violence policy as a starting point for developing a cyberspace policy. This strategy is a good one to the extent that the workplace violence policy has been successful. The "no tolerance" language has become popular in the workplace violence movement, with many organizations developing workplace violence policies stating that there would be no tolerance of violence within the organization. Such language has, at times, constrained managerial responses to cyber-misbehavior, such as by requiring the termination of an employee when it is not in the organization's best interest to terminate that person. Because the contextual variables relevant to instances of unacceptable behavior in cyberspace are even more varied and complex than those variables associated with violent behavior, it is critical that the policy not include the words "no tolerance."

When establishing policy, it is important for managers to consider the cultural perceptions of organizational affiliates, such as perceptions regarding the importance of sharing knowledge. It is also important to consider the assertion by Gackenbach, Guthrie, and Karpen (1998) that, in the context of its potential rewards and usefulness, the thrill of cyberspace can be seductive. As effective policy would protect the organization and affiliated individuals without unduly restricting or hamstringing affiliates' cyberspace behavior. An overly restrictive or time-consuming policy can limit productivity and encourage insiders to circumvent the policy, increasing risk behavior and providing rationalization strategies for violating the policy.

Specific Issues

Due diligence in hiring. A clear corporate policy regarding the assessment of risk factors when hiring is also critical.

The computer literacy possessed by most Generation X applicants increases the need to ask them appropriate cyberspace threat questions. Since it will be necessary to leverage the Web when hiring employees from Generation X (Bagby, 1998), applicants can be asked to provide a sample of their behavior in cyberspace. Samples of such behavior can be found in the electronic version of a resume and in e-mail correspondence with recruiting officials. These clues about whether the applicant understands ego boundaries appropriate in cyberspace should be considered when hiring.

Threat reporting mechanism. The creation of mechanisms insiders can use to report others' threat behaviors is critical to the success of any policy. Such policies must consider the American cultural prohibition against informing on one's colleagues. Overcoming this resistance may involve educating employees about the impact of betrayal of trust on all employees and discussing the concept that the identification and reduction of threats to the organization is not "snitching," but rather responsible organizational citizenship. Options for self-reporting with less serious consequences should also be encouraged for those who recognize that they are in the process of a seduction by a competitor or a criminal attempting to get access to organizational information.

Threat assessment, prevention, and intervention mechanisms. These mechanisms will most usefully involve a sharing of information among the critical partners discussed in the following section and the formation of a consensus among the partners regarding the level of threat and the selection of appropriate risk mitigation strategies. It is important that such a mechanism not be rigid, as organizational needs will change over time and even

potentially across insiders. For example, an organization may be willing to put up with increased threat from a researcher whose work is critical to organizational success, especially if the organization can develop strategies to reduce the risk of such threat.

Threat consideration when firing. The threat posed by former affiliates is a function of the amount of damage the former affiliate could do to the organization if he or she had the intent to do such damage. Treating employees with respect, even when firing them for heinous offenses, can significantly reduce such threats, as can providing outplacement assistance. Ensuring that an affiliate leaves the organization with as much self-respect intact as possible, and with employment options so that the future does not appear bleak, are important strategies for preventing cyber-retaliation. Other preventative measures involve ensuring that cyber access and plant access are terminated, but in a manner that is considerate of the individual's feelings. It is also critical to evaluate the extent to which the affiliate knows of vulnerabilities in the organization's information systems, and to immediately address those vulnerabilities.

Hibbard, McGee, and Wilder (1998) discussed additional countermeasures that employers can use to reduce risk: dividing information about trade secrets among employees, using non-compete and non-disclosure agreements, filing for trademarks and patents, and treating employees well. It is particularly important to make salaries competitive and to provide good job opportunities.

Other Issues

Security awareness. Dalton (1998) discussed the importance of training both information technology staff and end-users about security policies. Training should include not only the "do's and don'ts" of computer use, but all information relevant to cyberthreats and threat mitigation. Ways to evaluate the legitimacy of requests for information from outsiders, and issues regarding threats associated with joint ventures, should also be included in training. Information on where to report suspicious customers who may be seducing trusted insiders for their proprietary information should also be included.

Employee Assistance Programs (EAPs). With the exception of those who are seduced into betrayal and those who enjoy the thrill of it, the bulk of trusted insiders and former insiders who betray corporate trust might not do so if alternative coping strategies were available. A well-publicized EAP, staffed by licensed professionals, and for which use by employees carries no negative organizational consequences, can play a key role in helping trusted insiders develop coping strategies that reduce risk.

Specific additional groups which may be important in addressing cyberthreats merit additional comment.

Computer, physical and personnel security. The pool of trusted insiders and former trusted insiders does not include all the people who pose a risk to organizational information systems, but it is the pool over which psychologist-managers have influence. Forging partnerships with information and physical security professionals is critical because they have expertise that can help psychologist-managers deal with threat posed by trusted insiders. These partners will also play a key role in combating external threats to the organization's information. Personnel security professionals are likely not only to have the most up-to-date threat information, but also to possess threat assessment skills.

Law enforcement. Both local law enforcement authorities and the FBI are critical partners for employers facing cyberthreat concerns. For example, the FBI has created a security awareness program for companies that includes threat warnings. Such warnings include information about computer viruses and economic espionage threats and techniques. Over 25,000 companies belong to the program, which is called Awareness of National Security Issues and Response (ANSIR), and the services are free (The Thieves of Companies, 1998). The FBI urges companies to contact the FBI if they suspect corporate espionage. Local FBI offices are often willing to assist companies in developing prevention programs and with other security awareness initiatives. Information on contacting the local FBI can be found in the phone book or online at *http://www.fbi.gov*. The Web site contains other useful information, such as information on the ANSIR program and threat information.

Other critical partners. Other important partners include the organization's management and any oversight bodies. If the following are internal to the organization, they should also be included in policy determination, threat assessment, and risk mitigation when appropriate: human resources, mental health, legal, labor or union representatives, equal employment representatives, and any internal affairs departments, auditors, or ethics offices. Specific workplace violence prevention strategies are addressed in an excellent document entitled Dealing with Workplace Violence: A Guide for Agency Planners. This document is online at *www.opm.gov/workplac/index.html-ssi*. The recommendations can be easily adapted to address cyberspace threat.

Recommendations for Further Research

The present absence of research that clearly identifies the cyberspace risk factors and risk mitigators associated with an organization's trusted insiders leaves a gap in organizational risk management that the psychologist-manager is in a unique position to fill. It is critical that behavioral and interpersonal characteristics are considered, rather than just the technical factors associated with cyberspace betrayal of organizational trust. In the interim, the clinical and organizational skills of the psychologist-manager should be employed to adapt threat assessments of organization affiliates and organizational threat mitigation strategies to this emerging environment.

References

American Psychiatric Association. (1994). *Diagnostic and statistical manual of mental disorders* (4th ed.). Washington, DC: Author.

Aydin Corp. (1998, December 24). *Aerospace Daily, 188,* 472.

Bagby, M. (1998). *Rational exuberance.* New York: Dutton Plume.

Balsamo, A. (1995). Signal to noise: On the meaning of cyberpunk subculture. In F. Biocca, & M. R. Levy (Eds.), *Communication in the age of virtual reality* (pp. 347-368). Hillsdale, NJ: Erlbaum.

Biocca, F., & Delany, B. (1995). Immersive virtual reality technology. In F. Biocca, & M. R. Levy (Eds.), *Communication in the age of virtual reality* (pp. 57-124). Hillsdale, NJ: Erlbaum.

Biocca, F., & Levy, M. R. (Eds.). (1995a). *Communication in the age of virtual reality.* Hillsdale, NJ: Erlbaum.

Biocca, F., & Levy, M. R. (1995b). Virtual reality as a communication system. In F. Biocca, & M. R. Levy (Eds.), *Communication in the age of virtual reality* (pp. 15-32). Hillsdale, NJ: Erlbaum.

Dalton, G. (1998, August 31). Acceptable risks. *Information Week.*

Denning, D. E. (1999, April). Who's stealing your information? *Information Security,* p. 22.

Economic Espionage Act, 18 U.S.C.S. Section 1831. (Lexis 1999).

Ekman, P. (1992). *Telling lies: Clues to deceit in the marketplace, politics and marriage.* New York: Norton.

Foreign spies increase attacks on US companies, FBI reports. (1998, January 12). *Baltimore Sun,* 3A.

Gackenbach, J. (Ed.). (1998). *Psychology and the Internet: Intrapersonal, interpersonal, and transpersonal implications.* San Diego: Academic Press.

Gackenback, J., Guthrie, G., & Karpen, J. (1998). The coevolution of technology and consciousness. In J. Gackenbach (Ed.), *Psychology and the Internet: Intrapersonal, interpersonal, and transpersonal implications* (pp. 321-350). San Diego: Academic.

Goertzel, B. (1998). World wide brain: Self-organizing Internet intelligence as the actualization of the collective unconsciousness. In J. Gackenbach (Ed.), *Psychology and the Internet: Intrapersonal, interpersonal, and transpersonal implications* (pp. 293-319). San Diego: Academic Press.

Griffiths, M. (1998). Internet addiction: Does it really exist? In J. Gackenbach (Ed.), *Psychology and the Internet: Intrapersonal, interpersonal, and transpersonal implications* (pp. 61-75). San Diego: Academic Press.

Grohol, J. M. (1998). Future clinical

directions: Professional development, pathology, and psychotherapy on-line. In J. Gackenbach (Ed.), *Psychology and the Internet: Intrapersonal, interpersonal, and transpersonal implications* (pp. 111-140). San Diego: Academic.

Hafner, K., & Markoff, J. (1991). *Cyberpunks: Outlaws and hackers on the computer frontier.* New York: Simon & Schuster.

Harris, K. J. (1995). Computer crime: An overview. *Technical Bulletin, 1.* Sacramento California: SEARCH, The National Consortium for Justice Information and Statistics.

Hibbard, J., McGee, M. K., & Wilder, G. (1998, October 26). Top IT secrets—Businesses are taking steps to guard IT resources as the battle for key technology and top-notch talent keeps escalating. *Information Week.*

Igbaria, M., Shayo, C., & Olfman, L. (1998). Virtual societies: Their prospects and dilemmas. In J. Gackenbach (Ed.), *Psychology and the Internet: Intrapersonal, interpersonal, and transpersonal implications* (pp. 237-252). San Diego: Academic.

Janal, D. S. (1998). *Risky business.* New York: Wiley.

Joinson, Adam. (1998). Causes and implications of disinhibited behavior on the Internet. In J. Gackenbach (Ed.), *Psychology and the Internet: Intrapersonal, interpersonal, and transpersonal implications* (pp. 43-60). San Diego: Academic.

King, S. A., & Moreggi, D. (1998). Internet therapy and self-help groups—the pros and cons. In J. Gackenbach (Ed.), *Psychology and the Internet: Intrapersonal, interpersonal, and transpersonal implications* (pp. 77-109). San Diego: Academic.

Lane, C. A. (1997). *Naked in cyberspace: How to find personal information online.* Wilton, CT: Pemberton.

Levy, S. (1984). *Hackers.* New York: Bantam.

Lowman, R. L. (1994). *Counseling and psychotherapy of work dysfunctions.* American Psychological Association: Washington, DC.

A matter of life and death. (1999, January). *Information Security,* 55.

McKenna, J. T. (Ed.). (1997, January 20). National intelligence agencies. *Aviation Week and Space Technology, 146* (3), 61.

Meyer, K. (1995). Dramatic narrative in virtual reality. In F. Biocca, & M. R. Levy (Eds.), *Communication in the age of virtual reality* (pp. 219-258). Hillsdale, NJ: Erlbaum.

Mintz, H. (1999, April 11). Trade secrets case in San Jose, CA, may be prosecution blueprint. *San Jose Mercury News.*

Noonan, R. J. (1998). The psychology of sex: A mirror from the Internet. In J. Gackenbach (Ed.), *Psychology and the Internet: Intrapersonal, interpersonal, and transpersonal implications* (pp. 143-168). San Diego: Academic Press.

Nordwall, B. D. (1997, June 30). Cyber threats place infrastructure at risk. *Aviation Week and Space Technology, 146,* 51.

O'Shea, E. (1999, September). Revectoring society and business: The new order of electronic commerce. *IEEE Communications Magazine, 37* (9), 83-86.

Palmer, M. T. (1995). Interpersonal communication and virtual reality: Mediating interpersonal relationships. In F. Biocca, & M. R. Levy (Eds.), *Communication in the age of virtual reality* (pp. 277-302). Hillsdale, NJ: Erlbaum.

Pinkerton survey finds workplace violence greatest security risk. (1999, April). *Workplace Violence Prevention Reporter, 5,* 3.

Preston, J. M. (1998). From mediated environments to the development of consciousness. In J. Gackenbach (Ed.), *Psychology and the Internet: Intrapersonal, interpersonal, and transpersonal implications* (pp. 255-291). San Diego: Academic Press.

Reid, E. (1998). The self and the Internet: Variations on the illusion of one self. In J. Gackenbach (Ed.), *Psychology and the Internet: Intrapersonal, interpersonal, and transpersonal implications* (pp. 29-42). San Diego: Academic Press.

Shapiro, M. A., & McDonald, D. G. (1995). I'm not a real doctor, but I play one in virtual reality: Implications of virtual reality for judgements about reality. In F. Biocca, & M. R. Levy (Eds.), *Communication in the age of virtual reality* (pp. 323-345). Hillsdale, NJ: Erlbaum.

Simon, R. I. (1996). *Bad men do what good men dream.* Washington, DC: American Psychiatric Press.

Starr, B. (1997, September 17). 'Legal' espionage hits US high technology targets. *Jane's Defence Weekly, 28,* 8.

Theft of Trade Secrets Act, 18 U.S.C.S. Section 1832. (Lexis 1999).

The thieves of companies. (1998, December/January). *Working Woman, 22,* 24.

Turkle, S. (1984). *The second self: Computers and the human spirit.* London: Granada.

Turkle, S. (1995). *Life on the screen: Identity in the age of the Internet.* New York: Simon & Schuster.

Young, K. S. (1998). *Caught in the net: How to recognize the signs of Internet addiction and a winning strategy for recovery.* New York: Wiley.

[1] An earlier version of this paper was presented at the annual meeting of the Society of Psychologists in Management, Tampa, February, 1999. Opinions expressed in this article are those of the author and do not necessarily reflect those of the U.S. Government.

[2] *Correspondence to:*
Cathleen L. Civiello, Ph.D.
9936 Middle Mill Dr.
Owings Mills, MD 21117

The Psychologist-Manager Journal
1999, Vol. 3, No. 2, 167-179

Using the Internet and World Wide Web (WWW): Amazing Sites/Amazing Insights

Albert R. Hollenbeck[1,2,3]

AARP Research Group

This article explores an initial effort to create a research program for the World Wide Web (WWW) as an emerging media and business tool for a large non-profit membership organization. A framework for creating business knowledge in an Internet-based environment is outlined and discussed. The research plan that follows from that framework is outlined and our initial research experiences on the Internet are presented. This article also explores recent developments on the Internet and WWW that allow psychologist managers to network and organize information, and that make managers' and employees' work lives more efficient and effective.

The genesis for this article took place several years ago when, as often happens, two colleagues were sitting in an office sharing new experiences. Soon my supervisor walked by, stopped, and said, "You two are having too much fun to be working!" He then joined us for another hour of not working as we discussed new tools, sites, and techniques each of us had recently learned on and about the Internet and World Wide Web (WWW). At the conclusion of the session, we realized that our experience was worth sharing with others and so began quarterly "Amazing Things on the Web" seminars open to American Association of Retired Persons (AARP) employees. Each session had a format and followed a theme, such as looking at the strengths and weaknesses of different search engine algorithms (the programs that execute searches on the Internet), or examining the potential business application of a new technology or type of site. The sessions were always exciting, fun times for us and the participants[4] to explore and share (some of the

more interesting sites visited in the course of our explorations are described below).

Programmatic research on the WWW at AARP

These excursions into cyberspace have formed the nucleus for what has evolved into an ongoing emerging media research program at AARP. In June 1998, I was commissioned to create a research support team to provide assistance to AARP's Strategic Activity Team (SAT) on Emerging Media. The focus of "emerging media" was AARP's one and one-half year old presence on the WWW, *AARP Webplace, http://www.aarp.org.* In the several months that followed, I constructed a research team from a pool of internal AARP research staff and held a number of discussions with individuals about the SAT. It became clear to us that little was known about WWW research, either among my research team members or among the SAT members. Logic and aesthetic design sense had dictated the functions and form of *AARP Webplace* in its creation, but there were no data to determine whether goals had been achieved, and the SAT was fearful of making changes without knowing the consequences of those changes. Three directions were immediately obvious to us. First, the research team would need to educate itself on state-of-the-art WWW research. Second, our clients had an immediate, short-term need for research-based information to provide justification and context for imminent *AARP Webplace* changes. Finally, a long-term research program was needed to address emerging WWW research issues for AARP. What follows is a summary of how these challenges were addressed, the plan that emerged, and progress made to date.

A Practical Education In WWW Research

When our research team was forming, we quickly observed that none of us had any direct WWW research experience. No one knew very much about past WWW research other than that done on a few limited, topical areas that each of us may have explored. We soon discovered that no one else knew very much either. We found, in attempting to educate ourselves, that past knowledge did not exist in texts and journals. The Internet is both a medium to study and a repository of accumulated knowledge about itself. Unfortunately, the technology was advancing so rapidly that the usual sequence of knowledge creation and documentation was disrupted. There simply was almost no literature to master. Often what was written, including AARP's own research, was outdated by the time it was posted somewhere for retrieval.

In our efforts to understand current state-of-the-art Internet research, we searched widely. We networked among ourselves and with everyone who might have some knowledge about Internet research. We talked with consultants, vendors, our clients, and our colleagues. We read extensively, both traditionally and in the popular Internet trade publications, and on the Internet itself. We used AARP's Research Information Center and all its library resources. We searched and surfed the Internet for its hidden knowledge.

Not surprisingly, we found very little systematic scientific research and many issue debates about research-related topics, such as that revolving around Internet penetration rates in the general population. Early studies indicated that the typical Internet users were highly educated young males who were relatively affluent for their age. Our first study (Fisher, Tartaglione, Gann *et al.*, 1998)[5] confirmed this trend for visitors to *AARP Webplace*. By April 1999, a different study (Tartaglione, Privalsky *et al.*, 1999a)[5] employing the same sampling techniques but recruiting a different population found that the visitor-gender ratio had become more female than male, a trend mirroring Internet trends and the U.S. population in general.

As these examples illustrate, rapid change is making research on the Internet a very difficult task. We appear to be in the middle of a previously unexperienced cohort effect that is impacting the entire U.S. population in a short period of time. In this context, it may not be worthwhile to expend the resources to understand the change until Internet penetration starts to slow. The best we may able to do until then is to learn what we can through well-designed, cross-sectional studies, and to enjoy the rapid ride into the future.

Responding to Client Needs

One pragmatic task of any consultant, either external or internal, to an organization is to ensure that the client is a satisfied customer. A key to satisfying customers is to understand their perceived concerns and immediate needs and to deliver, promptly, services that resolve those concerns and satisfy those needs. In practice, this means a consultant is almost always working simultaneously on two fronts: the client's analysis of the problem, and the consultant's analysis. In this case, we began to work immediately on the client's problems while we educated ourselves on WWW research and created a framework for programmatic WWW research. Our client's immediate needs fell into two research categories: (1) user profiles of visitors to *AARP Webplace*; and (2) usability studies of the Internet as a medium to provide informational content to older adults.

Visitor profiling. Initially, we thought user profiling studies would be relatively simple and straightforward research designs. We were extremely naïve about the complexity of research issues that could be raised by even the simplest research design on the WWW.

Visitor profiling seemed to be one of the easiest studies to initiate, or so we thought. The Internet is an ideal medium for collecting information about itself and the people who use it. On the surface, the methodology appears to be simple and elegant—every third visitor was intercepted and invited to participate in a survey about *AARP Webplace*. If they declined, they were returned to *Webplace*; if they agreed to the survey, they were linked to another location on a different server that contained the specialized software for survey administration. Although this may sound like a simple, reasonable sampling strategy and a desirable way to collect data (because once set up on our servers, the entire process is automated, needing no human intervention), the practical realities were a little more complex.

Here is a short list and description of the problems the research strategy encountered:

- We identified more than 200 different browsers coming to *AARP Webplace*. Most were able to read the underlying programming language (Java), but many of the older browser versions could not.
- We found that each personal computer could be, and most likely was, configured slightly differently, making page layouts (fonts, colors, text-point size) variable and not under our control when received by the user.
- We found that different Internet service providers (ISPs) operate their servers differently, and the functionality available to their users may vary accordingly. For example, older versions of Web-TV and older browsers used by America Online (AOL) did not recognize Java, leaving these visitors in limbo, staring at a blank page when our automated invitation was displayed. We partially solved this problem by shrinking the invitation so it did not fill the entire screen, enabling users to simply close the invitation window.

Nevertheless, despite these and similar problems, we were able to complete a valid survey of 1,500+ visitors to *AARP Webplace*, profiling and baselining their visitor characteristics (Fisher, Tartaglione, Gann et al., 1998)[5].

As part of the profiling research, we attempted to develop a deeper understanding of visitor behavior by tracking individuals' movements while visiting *AARP Webplace*. The Internet was created by engineers and computer scientists steeped in systems theory who love to measure every aspect of system perform-ance from input to outputs (and every-thing in between). In theory, every time an individual visits a Web page hosted by a server, the server tracks that individual's visit—every page visited, every mouse click on a link, and every form entry sub-mitted. This would imply that managers could ask any reasonable question about visitor behavior, and track behavior from the entry to our home page to where they go after they leave us. All of these data presumably could be collected without Web site visitors even being aware that their behaviors were being monitored.

Real-life tracking efforts are not so straightforward. First, we found that everything was indeed tracked, but this process in turn generated incredible amounts of data. For example, less than a week's activity on *AARP Webplace* gener-ated over a gigabyte (10^9 bytes) of data. Our desktop computers and analysis packages were not designed to handle that volume. Second, there were a few prob-lems with the metrics—i.e., the way events were measured. For instance, the popular measure "hits" might be expected to be a count of the number of visitors to a Web page. In reality, "hits" are deter-mined by the number of visits to different elements on the same page, each location visited counting as a "hit." The underly-ing criteria of mutually exclusive and exhaustive categories was not met.

We then considered measuring how long each visitor stayed on a page. The duration a behavior lasts is usually an instructive behavioral measure and may be as important as behavioral frequencies. This approach also proved unexpectedly problematic.

Web page visitors are tracked individ-ually on the server hosting the page by what is known as an IP address (a numer-ic code identifying the originating com-puter so that the message units can be sent back and forth and tracked by the servers that transmit them). There are thus two basic problems in measuring visit dura-tion. First, because of the back-and-forth nature of the dialogue between the two server computers, one computer is wait-ing while the other is talking (machines, it seems, can be more courteous than peo-ple). The question then arises as to how long one computer waits. Many servers default to a wait time that is longer than the average person tends to stay on a Web page. There is a good reason for this. Message units are sent over the vast com-plexity of the Internet network. The per-son on the other end may be momentarily distracted, unable to respond (the reality may be that the visitor to the site got tired of waiting for the page to load and went on to do something else). Additionally, seemingly unique computer addresses may be coming from behind organization-al firewalls (server software that protects the server from unauthorized access) and have their IP addresses assigned by their Internet Service Provider's (ISP) server, or a firewall server, so that a new IP address is generated for each Internet ses-sion.

While these issues are more complex than would be desired, alternatives were suggested. The very volume in visitor traffic that creates one problem is also the solution of the other. There are tech-niques for sampling and estimating vari-ous parameters on Web page statistics and we discovered in this environment having a "theory" about visitor behaviors helps control the sheer volume of data. For those intrigued by these issues, our team has written a monograph (Privalsky *et al.,* 1999)[5]. Also, others (Novak & Hoffman, 1996) are calling for the standardization of Web page measurements to address these problems.

Usability studies. Usability study methodology developed in the systems engineering field (see Nielsen, 1993, for an overview) contains many elements familiar to research psychologists. In our context, usability testing involved bringing subjects (adults older than age 45) into a laboratory situation in which stimuli (Web pages and their elements) were presented to them via a computer in a controlled manner. Subjects were asked to perform systematic tasks using the computer and the stimuli. Their performances on these tasks were observed and videotaped for later analysis. Psychologists in an experimental laboratory might consider this work pre-research in that it is used to refine procedures, instrumentation, and protocols for later experimental work. In the systems approach, this pre-research is *the* research, in that what is learned is used to modify the system under study. Usability testing is primarily conducted with a small number of subjects (e.g., Kazdin, 1982; Robinson & Foster, 1979). Systems problems typically are identifiable after a few subjects use a system, and it is a usual and desirable practice to modify the system under study after early problem identification.

Our team immediately undertook two usability studies to address client needs and concerns with WWW-based pages (Grant *et al.,* 1999a, 1999b)[5]. The first project (Grant *et al.,* 1999a)[5] focused on a prototype Web page for a community calendar to be customized by listing local events of interest to AARP members. User perceptions and preferences were explored for: (1) general layout, organization, labels, and content; (2) event organization; (3) event content; and (4) search function. Direct observation of users identified a number of recommended changes for the Web page designers to consider. For example, users were offered three search options, or search tools, and then asked to find different types of information on the calendar. While analysis of the observational data indicated that most users favored one search tool, the majority of users found distinctions between types of searches, even if they did not correctly identify the most appropriate search tool (Grant *et al.,* 1999b)[5]. This finding led to a recommendation for revising the layout and improving the description of all search tools.

The second usability study focused on *AARP Webplace* (Grant *et al.,* 1999b)[5]. This project had goals similar to these of the community calendar, but focused on the larger, publicly available *Webplace.* A strength of usability testing is its ability to identify systemic problems. For example, in this study the paradox of providing large quantities of information on a Web site and also making particular information easy to find was highlighted. In one task, users were asked to "find out why Social Security benefits are adjusted every year." The answer was located in a document several pages removed from the home page, and there were multiple routes to locating this information. Only five of 30 users were able to find this information, and one of the problems was the multiplicity of search routes and potential links. Specifically, if users searched logically and went to the "Legislative Issues" page, they were confronted with six direct links to Social Security and more than 50 pages of content, plus a number of links to other "Social Security" sites. A simple search for the information yielded the correct answer as one of the listed search findings, but it was not readily identifiable because the listed content differed from the question asked. A sophisticated, experienced searcher might have noticed this connection, but most of the users tested did not. This told us that there is a great need to educate users on how search engines operate and what they need to look for in search results, as well as a need for search engine tools that are easier to use.

A Framework for Long-Term WWW Research

Arbnor and Bjerke (1997), in their book *Methodology for Creating Business Knowledge*, provide an overview of knowledge generation in today's business environment. Our team constructed its research plan incorporating Arbnor and Bjerke's three (1997) approaches to generating business knowledge: analytic, systems, and actors. The analytic approach is most familiar as the scientific paradigm, the systems approach as modern systems theory, and the actors approach as a constructionist dialectic view of reality. What was critical for our team's understanding was realizing that all three approaches co-exist in our organization, our clients, and ourselves, and there is value to be gained by employing each of the three methodologies. Psychologists will again recognize this as a variation of the familiar strategy of the classic multi-method, multi-trait matrix outlined by Campbell and Fiske (1967). In this case, paradigm boundaries are crossed to discover research methods, and it is recognized that truth, or concepts of reality, may differ for our many clients depending upon their paradigmatic perspective. What follows are descriptions of our use of these three approaches in advancing WWW research at AARP.

The Analytic Approach

The team's initial work focused on traditional research concerns of descrip-tion, experimentation, and methodology. In addition to our work on visitor profiling and understanding server measurement, we have now completed a study using a panel design that compared invited visitors' evaluations of *AARP Webplace* to those of three other WWW sites (Fisher, Tartaglione, Gross *et al.*, 1998)[5]. This study identified strengths and weaknesses of our Web site relative to the other sites. We have also completed a methodological study comparing a traditional phone survey with an online panel examining member views on a political issue, Social Security (Gross *et al.*, 1999)[5]. Few differences were detected, and those that were appeared to be caused by differences in the presentation of questions in visual versus auditory formats. Further analyses, yet to be done, could tell us whether or not these differences were due to population sampling differences (online vs. random telephone population). We have a second study (Tartaglione, Keenan *et al.*, 1999)[5] in the field comparing a telephone survey with an online survey on a topical area, adult learning. There is also methodological work on two surveys (Tartaglione, Privalsky *et al.*, 1999a, 1999b)[5] for which the data have just been collected examining drop-out patterns of those taking online surveys, especially looking for fatigue effects. We have discovered that, for our primary population of interest (those older than age 45) longer surveys (15 to 20 minutes) are not a problem, despite the fact that all of our current vendors for Web-based surveys report finding an upper limit of 15 minutes for surveys of the general population.

The Systems Approach

Our team has conducted three "systems" studies: two on specific Web page usability and one on search engine characteristics (Grant *et al.*, 1999c)[5]. The purpose of this the latter study was to identify a list of search words and search engines that would assist Web page designers in creating a site that would maximize page exposure to users conducting searches. This addresses the goal that AARP's Web site appear in Web search engines. This research was able to demonstrate that certain page structures can yield predictable results in any of the tested search engines. In this manner, a methodology has been developed to assess the impact of changes in Web page design on search results in various search engines over time.

The Actors Approach

A key difference of the actors approach from the other two knowledge-generation approaches is the assumption that reality is a construct actors create through their dialogue. While the process of dialogue and the constructs it creates can be the focus of research (i.e., research findings are an explication of all the different actors' points of view and their collective agreement becomes the data and business knowledge), we chose to use the actors approach as a heuristic instead of a research technique. This became a way for our team and the organization (our original internal clients, the internal research community, and our ever-expanding base of internal clients) to share knowledge and to define the reality of the WWW for the AARP. Thus, we established direct dialogue with clients and potential clients, published our research reports as a monograph series, and plan to hold AARP-wide presentations focusing on what we have learned from our research questions and about the process of conducting WWW research.

What We Have Learned So Far

In many ways, the work of me and my colleagues in this area has taken us to the a new world aptly described by William James (1890) as a "blooming, buzzing confusion." Nevertheless, today we know the WWW world (and also that of the infant) is more ordered than James' characterization, it is just ordered differently than our past experiences, and that with which we are familiar and comfortable. In a little over a year and a half spent researching the WWW and leading virtual teams, we have come to the following observations:

(1) The WWW is in a constant state of flux. It exists both as an entity to be studied for its own sake and as a medium for conducting research on multiple psychological topics. Phenomenologically, we are just starting to understand that it is altering, and will alter, the way we live our lives, as well as the social, economic, and technological forces that are driving its existence and evolution. Psychologist-managers, with their training in studying change in organizations, individuals, and environments are well-prepared analytically for studying the WWW. What they are not so well-prepared to assist with is the speed with which WWW changes are occurring. None of us has experience traveling at the present speed of change on the WWW.

(2) The WWW is a complex medium. Initially, we were naïve about the depth of this complexity. In the same way that the Internet is having an impact on our culture, it is having an impact on our world views. The technical environment of the WWW is a far cry from rats or pigeons pressing bars in cages that trip mechanical switches to record data; the bars and cages of the WWW are several magnitudes of sophistication more complex.

Simultaneously, the WWW is also much more powerful than the standard research tools with which we are used to exploring. For instance, there are some preliminary findings that panel surveys on the WWW yield a completion rate of roughly 20 percent immediately after the survey is launched, and have reached 80 percent completion within 48 hours. This type of almost instantaneous communication, coupled with the power to reach vast numbers of people, has to change the way we think about doing research. What we knew yesterday is not invalidated; we simply need to shift our thinking from what was impossible several years ago to what is possible and rather easy to do today. We have, however, found that making this shift is easier said than done.

(3) Psychologist-managers are well-positioned to deal with the future of the WWW. Most of us who have been psychologists for some time are at least familiar with the analytic, the systems, and the actor models described earlier. Individually, we may need to stretch our boundaries to feel comfortable in this new world that employs multiple explanatory models simultaneously, but psychology is a strong enough discipline to encompass all. The Society of Psychologists in Management (SPIM), as an organization of psychologists-managers, is proof that these boundaries can be stretched (Lowman, 1999).

Internet Tools and Practices for the Psychologist-Manager

In this final section of the article, I will explore some sites on the WWW likely to be of interest and enjoyment to the psychologist-manager, always mindful that even fun has potential managerial applications. Here I will examine specific WWW tools that may be of daily use to

psychologist-managers. The reader is encouraged to browse to the home page created for this presentation, *www.homestead.com/spim99*, as it provides direct links to all of the sites discussed.

"Fun" Sites on the WWW

The four sites (*MyCorkboard*, *WebFerret*, *Andy Bauch's Magic*, and *PeepingTom*) that we will explore in this category represent different or new technologies on the WWW that are enjoyable to use and that can be integrated into business applications.

MyCorkboard, http://www.mycorkboard.com, is a Web site that offers a free[6], downloadable screen saver program. This is not a typical screen saver, however. *MyCorkboard* is an interactive screen saver with multiple features useful on any desktop. For example, images from photographs to artwork may be custom-framed, and arranged on the desktop. The Web site offers a range of downloadable art and other tools to registered users. There is a "sticky note" feature that includes a "to do" list function. All of these are easily created, moved, and/or deleted from the desktop with simple right-mouse clicks. In a LAN environment, users of *MyCorkboard* have some limited interactive capability, such as playing harmless pranks on their colleagues. I have found *MyCorkboard* useful when visiting someone whom I know is a user and who I know is out of the office. I quickly pull up a "sticky note" and leave my message. From a business perspective, this is one of those computer applications that is weaning me away from my traditional desk to using my computer for former paper-and-pencil tasks.

WebFerret, http://www.ferretsoft.com /netferret/index.html, is a downloadable program that directly searches all the major search engines on the WWW. The program can link to any browser to examine search results; it is useful in cases in which the pop-up short description of each page does not provide enough information. *WebFerret* is extremely quick and, because it runs from your computer, is not dependent on a single search technology. Similar products, such as *WebTurbo* (*http://www.Webturbo.com*), are available as browser plug-in's, but they are dependent on their own site's server, which can suffer heavy demands and server outages. In a matter of minutes, we have used *WebFerret* to locate sites and information that others have spent days and weeks searching for via traditional search engines. If speed of information retrieval is one of your business concerns when using the WWW, then *WebFerret* is one solution.

Andy Bauch's Magic, *http://members.tripod.com/~andybauch/magic.html*, is included for potential business use to show how a "fun" site can be used to illustrate psychological principles. Here, the learning vehicle is a card trick in which the viewer receives a hand of cards, and then is asked to focus on a card of choice, after which the cards disappear, then reappear minus the chosen card. It is left to the reader to solve how the trick is performed and to discover the underlying principle (for a hint, psychology history buffs should consult Bruner and Postman, 1949).

The final site to be discussed in the "fun" category is *PeepingTom*, *http://www.coolbase.com/peepingtom/index.html*. Despite its name, and the fact that pornography on the Internet is a driving technological and financial force, *PeepingTom* long ago separated itself from prurient interests. Rather, *PeepingTom* is a window on the world providing links to most of the live video

cameras connected to the WWW The user of these links can, for example, find images of current traffic patterns around Washington, D.C., beach parking in the Netherlands, and rooftop views of many international cities. Some sites even offer remote control so that you can explore, within camera range, different views of a locale. This site is especially useful to those who do a lot of business traveling to new locations.

WWW Tools

The following collection of Web sites consists of tools we have found useful in our daily work lives. The first two sites are helpful communication tools. *PlanetAll*, *http://www.planetall.com*, is a Web-based address book with several unique features. After downloading special tools, *PlanetAll* allows users to synchronize with their desktop addressing systems, such as Microsoft's Outlook™, Outlook Express™, and others. A nice feature of this site is the ability to enter address changes at home, in the office, or over the Internet and then do a periodic synchronization so that the same information is created and updated simultaneously at all locations. Free software is also available for synchronization with Palm Pilots and other hand-held devices. In addition, *PlanetAll* allows for the creation of shared networks, enabling calendars and travel schedules to be shared among work group members.

Delphi Forums, *http://www.delphi.com*, is a companion site to *PlanetAll* that allows for the creation of a common group work space with shared discussion areas, Web page hosting, and online bulletin boards. *Delphi Forums* allow open or closed discussion areas and the ability to engage in either threaded discussions (wherein items and responses are linked in the sequence that they occur) and live chats. Enhanced capabilities and server space for forum (discussion group) hosting is available for a small fee. As the Internet has matured, a number of similar services, all with slightly different features, have emerged. Two worth exploring are *Anexa, http://www.paralogic.com*, which is similar to *Delphi Forums*; and *Visto, http://www.visto.com*, which takes a work-group/project-based approach to creating a shared online community. Specifically, *Visto* is designed especially for small work groups on any topic or project to share information and documents about that project. *Anexa* and *Visto* offer free services for groups of limited size with the hope that members will purchase their more advanced professional versions.

The next two sites are illustrative examples, among many now available on the Internet, for creating and hosting your own home pages for personal or professional uses. The most widely known of these is *Geocities, http://www.geocities.com*. *Geocities* offers free software editors to program Web pages, tutorials, and a community of several million, many of whom are willing to assist you in creating your own pages. For someone new to the Internet and its unique language and techniques, *Geocities* might be an imposing experience, but it is also a good place to learn first-hand how Web sites are created.

A different approach to creating Web pages is offered by *Homestead, http://www.homestead.com*. *Homestead* uses a Java editor program that loads on the computer while connected to the Internet. The program is interactive and provides layout features, text editing, and a host of buttons, icons, and Web page tools, such as visitor counters and guest books. Anyone familiar with current word-processing packages, such as Microsoft Word™ or WordPerfect™, should have no problems with the *Homestead* editor. To illustrate, for presenting these sites at the 1999 SPIM annual conference, I created a Web page on *Homestead* in about 15 minutes. The reader is referred there for a listing of links in the presentation and this paper (*http://www.homestead.com/spim99*).

The next two sites are for all those of us who relate to travel. Most readers are familiar by this time with the major commercial travel sites available on the Internet, such as Microsoft™ Expedia™, *http://www.expedia.com*. However, there are lesser known sites that can also provide useful information. One such site is *Metro, http://metro.ratp.fr:10001/bin/cities/english*. This free service, based in France, provides interactive maps and schedules for most of the world's major subway systems. For instance, if you are traveling in Munich and wish to take the subway from a downtown station to the Olympic Village, Metro provides directions, maps, and the anticipated travel time. Door-to-door directions can be found on another Web site, *Mapquest, http://www.tripquest.com*. *Mapquest* can give you free, specific, point-to-point directions and maps to follow in the United States and most European countries.

The next site must be introduced with a note of caution. *Bibliofind*[7], *http://www.bibliofind.com*, is a site designed for the used book trade, but fortunately for bibliophiles it is open and free to the public. *Bibliofind* is a service for used book dealers which allows them to upload their database of used books into a master file that may be searched by prospective buyers. Most used bookstores in the United States and Canada (and by some in the United Kingdom and

Australia) use this service. Be fore-warned, however, that accessing this site may be costly because users are likely to find all the books for which they have spent years searching, often available at discount prices. One colleague, for example, located several thousand dollars worth of books for which he had been searching for years. Direct orders may be placed on this site, and those not finding what they seek may put books on a personal watch. *Bibliofind* represents the Internet at its best.

The final site to be discussed in this section is a resource for the psychologist-manager who conducts research. Dan Blaine is an educational psychologist at the University of Hawaii who has organized his bookmarks by topic and shared them with the online community at the following Web site: *http://www2.hawaii .edu/~daniel/bkmrks.html*. Major research categories include: advanced topics, statistics, measurement and evaluation, research applications, mathematical, qualitative, and data collections. This is an extensive collection taking more than 35 pages to print.

This particular collection of Web sites represents just a few of those that have proved particularly useful to me and my AARP colleagues. Of course, the WWW is constantly changing and every arena is now very competitive. By the time this article appears in print, many of the sites presented will have undergone major changes. Also, the WWW is evolving to meet the needs of increasingly sophisticated users. Thus, in the future, what we see as marvels today will be considered mundane and archaic as they are replaced by newer technologies.

References

Arbnor, I. & Bjerke, B. (1997). *Methodology for creating business knowledge, 2nd edition.* London: Sage.

Bruner, J.S. & Postman, L. (1949). On the perception of incongruity: A paradigm. *Journal of Personality, 18,* 206-23.

Campbell, D.T. & Fiske, D.W. (1967). Convergent and discriminant validation by the multitrait-multimethod matrix. In D.N. Jackson, & S. Messick (Eds.) *Problems in human assessment.* New York: McGraw-Hill.

Fisher, L., Tartaglione, R., Gann, D., Hollenbeck, A., Grant, G., Privalsky, M., & Steele, C. (1998, October). *Visitor profile and evaluation of AARP Webplace: A survey of AARP Webplace visitors by the NPD Group, Inc.* (Emerging Media Research Support Team Monograph No. 1). Washington, DC: AARP.

Fisher, L., Tartaglione, R., Gross, S., Moncayo, G., Aloia, D., Robinson, B., Hollenbeck, A., Grant, G., Privalsky, M., & Steele, C. (1998, December). *AARP Webplace versus other sites: Web site comparison study by NFO, Inc.* (Emerging Media Research Support Team Monograph No. 4). Washington, DC: AARP.

Grant, G., Hollenbeck, A., Fisher, L., Tartaglione, R., Privalsky, M., Steele, C., Gross, S., Moncayo, G., & Robinson, B. (1999a, September). *AARP community calendar prototype user testing project—A report on ten community calendar user tests by Frank N. Magid Associates, Inc.* (Emerging Media Research Support Team Monograph No. 3). Washington, DC: AARP.

Grant, G., Hollenbeck, A., Fisher, L., Tartaglione, R., Privalsky, M. Steele,

C., Gross, S., Moncayo, G., & Robinson, B. (1999b, September). *AARP Webplace user testing—A report on 30 AARP Webplace user tests by Frank N. Magid Associates, Inc.* (Emerging Media Research Support Team Monograph No. 6). Washington, DC: AARP.

Grant, G., & Hollenbeck, A., Fisher, L., Tartaglione, R., Privalsky, M., Steele, C., Gross, S., Moncayo, G., & Robinson, B. (1999c, October). *AARP's presence on Internet search engines—AARP Internet search engine baseline technical report by Eagle Research Laboratories* (Emerging Media Research Support Team Monograph No. 7). Washington, DC: AARP.

Gross, S., Moncayo, G., Aloia, D., Fisher, L., Hollenbeck, A., Tartaglione, R., Grant, G., Privalsky, M., Steele, C., Robinson, B. & The Social Security Support Team. (1999, January). *AARP members' views of Social Security: A methodology comparison—The AARP online Social Security survey: A survey of members of AARP by Louis Harris and Associates versus a telephone survey of members by FGI, Inc.* (Emerging Media Research Support Team Monograph No. 5). Washington, DC: AARP.

James, W. (1890). *The principles of psychology (2 vols.).* New York: Holt.

Kazdin, A.E. (1982). *Single-case research designs.* New York: Oxford University Press.

Lowman, R.L. (1999). A sense of place. *The Psychologist-Manager Journal, 3,* 119-120.

Nielsen, J. (1993). U*sability engineering.* New York: Academic Press.

Novak, T.P. & Hoffman, D.L. (1996, September). New metrics for new media: Toward the development of Web measurement standards. *Project 2000: www2000.ogsm.vanderbilt. edu.*

Privalsky, M., Hollenbeck, A., Grant, G., Fisher, L., Steele, C., Tartaglione, R., & Gross, S. (1999, March). *AARP Webplace: Analysis of internet server log files—research implications and future directions* (Emerging Media Research Support Team Monograph No. 2). Washington, DC: AARP.

Robinson, P.W. & Foster, D.F. (1979). *Experimental psychology: A small-n approach.* New York: Harper & Row.

Tartaglione, R., Privalsky, M. & Hollenbeck, A., Fisher, L., Steele, C., Gross, S., Moncayo, G., Grant, G., Aloia, D., Crepeau, M., & Robinson, B. (1999a, September). *Interests and characteristics of potential online learners—A survey of AARP Webplace visitors by Ronin Corporation* (Emerging Media Research Support Team Monograph No. 8). Washington, DC: AARP.

Tartaglione, R., Privalsky, M. & Hollenbeck, A., Fisher, L., Steele, C., Gross, S., Moncayo, G., Grant, G., Aloia, D., Crepeau, M., & Robinson, B. (1999b, September). *Interests and characteristics of potential AARP member online learners—A survey of AARP Webplace visitors by the NPD Group* (Emerging Media Research Support Team Monograph No. 9). Washington, DC: AARP.

Tartaglione, R., Keenan, T. & Hollenbeck, A., Fisher, L., Gross, S., Crepeau, M., Reaser, J., Stromberg, K., & Robinson, B. (1999, October). *Older adult preferences for how they learn—A national survey of adults age 50 and older by Harris Interactive, Inc.* (Emerging Media Research Support Team Monograph No. 10). Washington, DC: AARP.

[1]Portions of this paper were presented at the 15th annual SPIM Conference, Tampa, FL, February, 1999. The views presented here are those of the author and do not necessarily represent the policies or viewpoints of AARP.

[2]My colleagues and equal contributors in spirit to all that is here are Joel Reaser, Ph.D. and Hugh O'Connor, both, at the time, Associate Directors of Research, AARP Research Group and AARP's Emerging Media Research Support Team who are identified for each project in the reference list. The blame for any shortcomings, however, is wholly my own.

[3]*Correspondence to:*
Albert R. Hollenbeck, Ph.D.
AARP Research Group
601 E Street, N.W.
Washington, D.C. 20049
E-mail: ahollenbeck@aarp.org

[4]The original links from this presentation may be found on the WWW at *http://www.homestead.com/spim99*.

[5]At the present time, this monograph is a proprietary working document of AARP and not available for distribution.

[6]An additional tradition that was not always adhered to in the Seminars, but will be followed here, is that the sites we discuss are all "free" sites on the WWW. That is, the sites themselves, their services, and often their downloadable files are provided at no dollar cost to those who register. However, as we all know, there is often more than one way in which one "pays," such as by receiving constantly changing advertising on a site.

[7]While this paper was being drafted, *Bibliofind* was purchased by *Amazon.com*. The site still functions as described.

································

Personal Challenge

Getting the Best Out of Your Best People

································

Executive assessments, development and coaching

executive team building

merger integration   **succession planning**

cross-cultural development   **conflict resolution**

executive education

As management psychologists, RHR International spends a lot of time assessing and developing your best people. Everyday, we help companies throughout the world build effective and competitive organizations. For more information on how RHR International can help you meet your personal challenges, visit our web site at www.rhrinternational.com or call Jeff Durocher at 630. 766. 7007.

R H R
International

The Leaders in Leadership Development

The Psychologist-Manager Journal
1999, Vol. 3, No. 2, 181-190

Technological Innovations and Advancements for Psychologists Working With Organizations[1]

Carl I. Greenberg[2]
Assessment Solutions Incorporated

Information technology is rapidly becoming an integral part of the practice of industrial/organizational (I/O) psychology. This article reviews the relevant computer and telecommunications technologies, including applications in the areas of personnel assessment and selection and organization development (OD). The potential benefits are contrasted with the concerns such techniques raise in ensuring that fundamental psychometric properties are maintained.

Until recently, industrial/organizational (I/O) psychology had done little as a discipline to incorporate the rapid growth of technology. Certainly the advent of computers has greatly increased our productivity with regard to quantitative data analysis, but their application to the areas of personnel assessment and organizational development has been rare. Indeed, it could be argued that the biggest technological advancement that has been regularly applied to I/O psychology over the last 30 years is the "bubble sheet," i.e., machine-readable answer/scoring sheets.

Today, technology is making rapid inroads into the practice of I/O psychology, and will continue to do so for the foreseeable future. Indeed, it will not only provide the opportunity to offer faster service to organizations, but to all units regardless of their geographic locations around the world. Technology will also change the way psychologists practice and manage, and what we do for organizations. It will be the great enabler, further democratizing organizations and thus creating new and different organizational challenges.

Change will continue to be very rapid. By the time this article is printed and read, some innovations will be standard practice. Others will be discarded, only to be replaced by newer, more effective technological advances. This trend is evident in the consumer technology marketplace. For example, consumers are now replacing their analog cellular phones with digital ones. Consider how recently developed was the first cellular phone, and even the first portable home phone.

So rapid is the application of technology to our field that traditional methods of inquiry for writing such an article as this do not work. At first, I found myself researching this topic the traditional way—going to *Psychological Abstracts* to do a literature search. I conducted computer searches of research articles on how technology is being used by psychologists in organizations but found very little relevant to the topic. The most fruitful method by which to gather information was networking with colleagues. Another successful method was "following the money"—i.e., seeking out Web sites that sell technological applications of psychology and reading advertisements in human resource publications.

Technology Defined

The technology to be discussed here does not just concern computers. In recent years computers have become intertwined with telecommunications. Information and communications technologies are no longer distinct. This is most clearly demonstrated in the business world by recent mergers, acquisitions and strategic partnerships. AT&T, for example, is now quickly becoming the largest television cable company. Cable companies are offering high-speed Internet connections. America Online™, the largest Internet service provider, is forming partnerships with the large regional telephone companies (e.g., "America On Line", 1999). Computer software companies are selling their software over the Internet through online downloads. Hand-held organizers (e.g., Palm Pilot™) and digital cellular phones are now being advertised as having the capability to send and receive e-mail and other forms of information. Digitization of voice, video, and computer software (Negroponte, 1995) is making it commonplace for businesses and consumers to communicate inexpensively and reliably over the Internet. It will also become common practice to collect and access information via the Internet (or internally through an organization's intranet), through either public or privately secured web sites.

Technology and the Practice of Psychology in Organizations

Futurist John Naisbitt, in his prophetic book *Megatrends* (1984), discussed the impact of technology on human interaction. He posited that, as technology becomes a major part of mainstream society, people would have a greater desire for human interaction and humanistic undertakings. He coined this compensatory process "High Tech-High Touch" (Naisbitt, 1984). As we move from an industrial to an informational society, our need for human contact becomes greater. This is reflected in economic trends. The strong growth of the technological sector has been followed by that of the burgeoning customer service industry.

We have seen the shift to a more person-centered approach to organizational psychology. We used to communicate to clients about "personnel requirements" and knowledge, skills, and abilities ("KSA's"), now we label these "competencies." Psychologists formerly focused mostly on developing cognitive ability measures to predict organizational success; increasingly, they now examine constructs such as emotional intelligence (Goleman, 1998). Performance was traditionally measured through supervisory appraisals; now it has been somewhat democratized, with 360-degree surveys by which subordinates, customers, and peers have input in the appraisal process. Management training previously centered on teaching people how to manage things; now the focus is on how to lead people (Moxley and Wilson, 1998). Organizational research was formerly devoted to organizational behavior; now organizational values (e.g., Senge, 1990) are equally important. In short, it appears that as new technology has been applied to the practice of psychology in the workplace, the practice of psychology in the workplace has become more in touch with the whole person. Herein lies the value that psychologists potentially bring to organizations: they can recognize and intervene with the human issues associated with rapid advances in technology. In the following sections I will discuss the role of workplace psychology as technology pervades the traditional practice areas of employment processing, testing and assessment, and organizational development.

Technology and Employment Processing

The implementation of technological solutions has the most benefit in situations where the process is frequent and repetitive, and has a short cycle time. This is readily evident in the use of computer technology to perform accounting and manufacturing operations previously performed by employees. Today, this automation is also spreading to large companies with regard to their employment processes.

The recruiting of job candidates, especially in tight labor markets, becomes an ever-increasing challenge. A new channel from which to source job applicants is the Internet. Most companies with Web sites post job openings. University Web sites also list job openings for those companies involved in campus recruiting.

Among the most utilized services available on the Internet are those offered by commercial sites that are nothing more than electronic "help wanted" sections with the added ability to perform keyword searches. Web sites such as *www.monster.com* and *www.hotjobs.com* are examples of the more popular of these.

Job seekers can also place their resumes on the Internet. Many executive and professional search firms currently solicit registration of resumes online through their Web sites (e.g., *www.futurestep.com, www.laicompass. com,* and *www.mrinet.com*). Of course, anyone savvy enough to create a web page can place his or her resume on the Internet and, for a fee, have it registered

with a search engine (a Web site that allows keyword searches, such as *www.yahoo.com, www.altavista.com*).

For high-volume hiring situations, especially in jobs with high turnover, the need to continuously capture viable applicants is critical for the employment process to be successful. The linking of telephony with computers through what is called Interactive Voice Response (IVR) systems (Montdragon, 1999) has proven effective in these situations.

In a typical IVR employment process, interested job seekers call a toll-free number and make an initial employment inquiry. The pre-recorded message provides information important to the prospect, including the type of position openings available, hours of work, wage ranges, and essential job duties and responsibilities. Job seekers are often required to answer, using the telephone touch pad, some fundamental questions about their background, such as highest education level attained, whether or not they are licensed to drive a motor vehicle, and their amount of relevant job experience.

As job seekers respond to questions about themselves and their job preferences, they are channeled to different parts of the IVR script. If a job seeker, for example, is interested in a customer service representative position in Grand Rapids, Michigan, the IVR script will present specific information about the pay and working hours available at that location. If job seekers are found to meet basic job requirements they are given options for scheduling an appointment for further screening and interviewing at the employment office. Directions to the office are also provided.

The benefits of such a system to a high-volume employment operation are enormous. Technology increases the efficiency of the operation. No longer are people needed to do this repetitive, time-consuming work. Multiple job-seekers can access the system simultaneously 24 hours a day, seven days a week. Job-seekers can also call back and change their appointments without fear of leaving a poor first impression with someone in the employment office.

The employment operation now has a systematic database on its recruitment population. These data can be analyzed to determine when people are hanging up the phone, indicating loss of interest in the job. Is it the working hours, the pay, or the job duties that are causing people to lose interest in a certain position? Moreover, asking job seekers where they found out about the opening can help the employment office focus its recruitment efforts in ways that are most effective. For example, my own company recently analyzed the recruiting source data for one of our clients. We found that although Newspaper A produced the greatest number of responses to the job advertisement, Newspaper B produced a significantly higher rate of qualified candidates. The obvious conclusion for the client was to shift more advertising dollars to Newspaper B.

Testing and Assessment

Whether intended for employment, promotion, or individual development, assessment processes are moving away from traditional paper-and-pencil and live, face-to-face formats. Telecommunications and computer technology applications are becoming prevalent. These are discussed below.

Computer-Based Assessments

Personal computers were first seen as a panacea for the problems inherent to traditional paper-and-pencil tests. But computer-based assessments have not proliferated as rapidly as had been expected. It is still cost-effective to administer paper-and-pencil tests in controlled group-testing sessions. The cost of replacing such tests with a personal computer for each applicant, and ensuring the testing software will continue to work on newer models, is still prohibitive for most companies. For example, in the 1980's one company of the author's acquaintance invested heavily in creating cognitive ability tests for the computer, only to abandon the practice last year when the software would not run on contemporary operating systems.

Nevertheless, the personal computer is useful in the application of personnel assessments. One of its early uses was to gauge administrative skills, particularly typing, data entry, and word-processing. Computerized tests provide a reliable method of scoring and timing the test administration. In addition, stimuli can be presented in either a written (as with traditional typing tests) or auditory manner. The latter is especially important for jobs requiring information input from a telephone conversation or the transcription of dictated material.

Multimedia software (the integration of audio, video, animation, and written stimuli) allows for the creation of job simulations, particularly for jobs that require using a computer and performing a variety of tasks simultaneously. Here, job candidates are exposed to fictitious customers and co-workers and may be required to input information, make decisions, choose among a set of alternative behaviors, and search reference material. Different responses to a situation can then generate unique reactions from the computer, to which the candidate will have to again respond. The interaction continues until the situation is resolved.

Customer-service jobs are the group for which this test method is most commonly used. These tests are appealing because they simulate the job in a way that is attention- grabbing and engages the job candidate. However, some of the products on the market focus more on the stimuli than on the validity of behaviors measured, evidence for which may be sorely lacking. Test purchasers, especially business managers, who are not versed in the criteria for a quality employment selection test, are attracted to the face validity of the presentation and fail to assess the fundamental psychometrics of the instrument. *Caveat emptor* governs the current market.

Psychologists are required to follow stringent standards when developing, marketing and using assessment tools (American Educational Research Association [AERA], American Psychological Association [APA], National Council on Measurement in Education [NCME], 1999). Psychologists with appropriate training can provide invaluable assistance to organizations in selecting appropriate assessment tools and providing training in their use and interpretation.

Internet-Based Assessment Methods

Currently, the biggest trend in testing technology involves use of the Internet. Corporate human resource departments view this as a cost-effective way to screen job applicants across the world. By accessing secure Web sites, job applicants can complete a variety of tests and questionnaires that can be quickly scored and acted upon by a distant employment operation. The Internet allows for all types of computer-based testing to be administered without the need for the software to be in place at the testing site.

On the surface, this methodology seems ideal, but there are a few barriers to overcome. It is very important to ensure that the individual taking the test is truly the candidate. Allowing applicants to complete these tests at home may be administratively desirable for the employment office, but such an arrangement offers minimal test security. There must be some means of assurance that the job candidate is taking the test under structured test administration conditions and does not have access to resources that could aid in test performance (e.g., other people, reference material, etc.)

Timed tests, such as measures of cognitive ability, pose an additional obstacle. Internet connections are notoriously unreliable with regard to speed and stability. A number of solutions are available to overcome the varying speed of Internet connections. One elegant approach is to download the test in the computer's temporary memory (RAM), and thus use the computer's internal clock to measure time. A more sophisticated solution being used is to employ an algorithm that computes time adjustments based upon the response speed of the Internet connection.

Test security is also a major obstacle to valid employment testing on the Internet. Even if the job candidate can take a test via the Internet, there are no assurances that screens showing the test would not be printed off and distributed to other potential job candidates, or worse, placed on the Internet for the world to see. Test publishers are extremely hesitant to put their proprietary tests on the Internet, even over secure Web sites, since misuse or widespread distribution of the test can seriously compromise its appropriate use.

Despite advances in technology, it seems that for the immediate future the use of the Internet for test administration will be limited by the security of the venue. Companies using this medium for employment testing have created test administration site networks, such as through community colleges. Test-proctoring technology will be required before Internet testing is likely to be more widely accepted.

The Internet has also created a new set of issues for psychologists. It has democratized the development and distribution of tests. Anyone who wants to develop a test can do so and place it on the Web for anyone else to use. Goldberg (1999) has created a web site (*www.ipip.ori.org*) for the development of non-proprietary broad-based personality tests. This web site includes over 1400 test items for use by both the scientific and business communities. It also serves as a repository for validity studies using the database of test items. One commercial application of a test web site is *www.test.com*. For a fee, users can take an intelligence or personality test. The web site accepts tests from anyone, including psychologists (which raises the question of professional ethics). Without doubt, some employers have found this site and are using it to assess job candidates. Again, the dictum of *caveat emptor* seems relevant.

Communications-Based Assessment Methods

The simple telephone is an early, yet underutilized, technological enhancement for assessment. Many people have experienced a job interview over the phone. Interviews can range from off-the-cuff, unstructured exchanges conducted by a hiring manager, to formal, structured interviews that closely resemble personality tests, administered by trained assessors or psychologists. Clearly, the telephone is a cost-effective method for collecting vital information on prospective job candidates.

Conducting job simulation exercises over the phone is an effective method of measuring job-related competencies, especially in the growing customer-service sector. For example, Assessment Solutions Incorporated (the author's employer) has developed procedures for applying the assessment center method to telephone role-play assessments in order to screen customer sales and service job candidates.

The integration of telephony and the Internet with real-time video is creating a new market for remote role-play assessments. Higher fidelity assessments now can be constructed using video-mediated communication devices. For the price of an additional personal computer, real time two-way video communication is now available via high-speed communication lines (e.g., through cable modem or digital subscriber telephone lines) and a small camera on top of the computer monitor.

The content validity of role-plays conducted over the telephone has generally been limited to jobs in which incumbents conduct a significant amount of their work over the phone. With the economy of video-mediated communication devices, remote assessments are starting to emerge for jobs that are primarily performed face to face. Thus, from a remote location job simulations and interviews can be conducted where the assessor and the job candidate see and hear each other. Add to this dynamic the exchange of information over the Internet, and one has significantly cut expenses by eliminating the need to transport job candidates to an assessment location. Upgrading the fidelity of assessments from audio to video may also improve applicants' perceptions of the assessment process. Habash (1999) has shown the positive effects of video-mediated communication on decision-making groups.

Organizational Development Applications

Personal computers. PC software has made survey research a much easier task than in years past. Many software packages allow one to construct survey instruments, analyze data, and, most importantly, produce client-ready reports complete with bar charts and graphs. For example, SPSS, Inc. and The SAS Institute, Inc. offer a wide array of software packages that perform these functions.

Employee attitude surveys are the focus of most of these packages. Some packages come with survey item banks, so that with the click of a mouse survey items can be chosen. The ease in producing and analyzing surveys represented by such features can certainly save time for the professional. However, they can also lead to situations in which persons with no training in survey research methodology are conducting surveys for their organizations or consulting clients. The technical aspects of survey sampling and interpreting survey results are not handled by the software, and therefore it can lead to the production of an inconclusive and/or misleading product by the novice user.

Performance appraisal instruments, and 360° surveys in particular, have proliferated in the software market (Fried, 1998). Numerous companies advertising on the Internet and in human resources magazines sell computer programs that claim to design, analyze, and track the administration of multi-rater survey processes. Those who have had to shepherd the administration of a 360° survey process will find such software a time-saver. Many of these multi-rater approaches have not established adequate validity and reliability scores in accordance with professional standards (AERA, APA, NCME, 1999). Further,

these standards require that localized validity and reliability be established where the population being studied differs significantly from the population originally used to establish the instrument's validity and reliability. Such a difference is often present when industries or organizational types are different.

Internet-Based OD Procedures

Web site survey administration is quickly replacing the need for paper-and-pencil survey instruments. In organizations in which employees have Internet access, survey respondents only need to point and click on their responses and then instantly send the survey off for tabulation. It is a quick and efficient way to conduct surveys.

More and more of us are being sent surveys via the Internet. In the span of just a month, for example, I received three e-mail surveys, all from well-meaning graduate students on various professional and practice-related topics. As e-mail users become inundated with these surveys, as they now are with junk e-mail, these surveys will be automatically thrown away with the click of the mouse. Of course, this non-response information must also be included in response rate calculations when reporting on e-mail-based studies.

The effect of administering surveys over the Internet, especially employee surveys for which anonymity is crucial to the validity of the data, needs to be researched. It is quite possible for online questionnaires to be traced back to individual respondents. Just as organizations can monitor the Web sites that employees access while on the job, so too can they link the responses of a survey back to a particular person, raising ethical issues (see, e.g., Lowman, 1998). Even though software now on the market is said to ensure anonymity, respondents' lack of trust and perception of being traced may persist. The trade-off between employees' perceptions that they might lose anonymity versus the ease of administration and speed of reporting results needs to be weighed before making the decision to use a high-technology approach. Nonetheless, the Internet can be a good medium for fast, temperature-taking surveys on specific, non-threatening issues.

The Internet is also fast becoming the medium of choice for conducting 360° surveys, as seen by the proliferation of companies offering this service (see advertisements in human resource magazines and exhibit booths at human resource conferences). Anonymity is a major problem with such surveys. Raters are clearly identified on return forms for tracking purposes. The real benefit of conducting these surveys over the Internet is the ability to administer the process quickly and efficiently. For example, automatic reminder e-mails can be sent to raters who have yet to complete the survey. Moreover, as additional raters are needed for an individual ratee they can be sent a questionnaire within seconds. Feedback reports can be produced as soon as all the surveys for a ratee are returned.

Use of Telephony in OD

IVR can be an effective method of collecting survey information on specific issues. Short surveys can be created, administered and tabulated with a very short cycle time. Some IVR systems can automatically randomly sample and call employee telephone numbers. Those who answer the phone follow simple instructions and answer a few questions by pressing keys on the telephone touchpad. Those not answering the phone are left a voice-mail message asking them to call a telephone number and complete the survey.

Organizations find this technique useful for single-issue opinion gathering. For example, immediately after an announcement is made regarding organizational change, employee reactions can be assessed. What used to take weeks can now be accomplished in a matter of hours. Geographically dispersed organizations also find this an efficient way to collect survey data. However, respondent anonymity is a concern with this method as well, thus limiting its utility to non-threatening employee issues.

Use of Video Technology in OD

One of the largest expenses in developing multi-issue surveys is the travel associated with conducting face-to-face focus groups. Organizations equipping their members with video-mediated communication devices attached to their personal computers can now conduct remote focus groups or individual interviews, with the communication fidelity required to met the needs of both participant and facilitator.

Conclusions

Technology is developing faster than our practice field has usefully accommodated it. Personal computer software now entering the marketplace is being replaced rapidly by Internet-based applications. As the Internet becomes a primary source of information and way of conducting business, more of our services will be provided via this medium. The democratization of information distributed over the Internet (Freedman, 1999) has and will continue to create great opportunities for us as professionals. The services we provide organizations, as internal or external consultants, will be delivered faster, be more highly customized to clients' needs, and be more inclusive of remote organizational locations. Our ability to provide services more efficiently while maintaining high professional standards will greatly enhance the psychologist-manager's value to organizations.

Caution is warranted, however. Simply because a product or service uses the most advanced technology does not make its content superior. One has no guarantees that the computer software or Internet application one is using has the fundamental integrity to perform as advertised. As with any product or service, the buyer needs to ascertain the quality of what he or she is purchasing. A consumer, or the consultant of a consumer, of these products must be sure to research their content. If it is a test, has it been validated? If it is survey software, have the statistical formulas been properly developed and validated?

Data security is another concern. If test and survey data are being collected, where do they reside? Who has access to the data? How can an organization be sure that hackers internal and external to the organization are not compromising Internet applications (see Civiello, 1999, for a comprehensive treatment of this issue)?

Finally, one has to weigh the lifespan of the technology. The most advanced computer on the market will rapidly be replaced by something bigger, faster, and cheaper. Technology purchases made today will have a very short lifespan. As computer-based and communications-based technologies continue to merge, lifespan cycles are compressing rapidly.

References

America Online gains 2nd high speed access deal. (1999, March 11). *Newsbytes News Network. World Wide Web: http://www.newsbytes.com.*

American Educational Research Association, American Psychological Association, National Council on Measurement in Education (1999). *Standards for educational and psychological testing.* Washington, DC: American Psychological Association.

Civiello, C.L. (1999). Cyberspace, trusted insiders, and organizational threat: The role of the psychologist manager. *The Psychologist-Manager Journal, 3,* 146-166.

Fried, N.E. (1998, December). 360-degree software vendor shootout: Comparing needs and features. *HR Magazine,* pp. 8-13.

Friedman, T.L. (1999). *The lexus and the olive tree.* New York: Farrar, Straus & Giroux.

Goldberg, L. R. (1999). A broad-bandwidth, public-domain, personality inventory measuring the lower-level facets of several five-factor models. In I. Mervielde, I. Deary, F. De Fruyt, & F. Ostendorf (Eds.), *Personality Psychology in Europe,* Vol. 7. (pp. 7-28). Tilburg, The Netherlands: Tilburg University Press.

Goleman, D. (1998). *Working with emotional intelligence.* New York: Bantam Books.

Habash, T.F. (1999). The impact of audio or video conferencing and group decision tools on group perception and satisfaction in distributed meetings. *The Psychologist-Manager Journal, 3,* 211-230.

Lowman, R. L. (1998). *The ethical practice of psychology in organizations.* Washington, D.C.: American Psychological

Association.

Mondragon, N.J. (1999). Should we be driving technology solutions or just be passengers for the ride? A positive look at our field and technology. *The Industrial-Organizational Psychologist, 37,* 42-50.

Moxley, R. S. & Wilson, P.O.(1998). A systems approach to leadership development. In C.D. McCauley, R.S. Moxley, & E. Van Velsor (Eds.), *The center for creative leadership handbook of leadership development.* San Francisco: Jossey-Bass.

Naisbitt, J. (1984). *Megatrends: Ten new directions transforming our lives (Revised edition).* New York: Warner Books.

Negroponte, N. (1995). *Being digital.* New York: Knopf.

Senge, P.M. (1990). *The fifth discipline: the art and practice of the learning organization.* New York: Doubleday.

---

[1]An earlier version of this paper was presented at the annual meeting of the Society of Psychologists in Management, Tampa, February, 1999.

[2]*Correspondence to:*
Carl I. Greenberg, Ph.D.
ASI, 8000 Maryland Ave., Suite 820
St. Louis, MO 63105
E-mail:
greenberg@asisolutions.com

The Psychologist-Manager Journal
1999, Vol. 3, No. 2, 191-195

Case Study: Traditional Facilitation Skills Combined with Group Decision Technologies

Robert Cryer, Jr., & Albert R. Hollenbeck[1,2]
AARP Research Group

This paper follows the journey of a team of facilitators as they attempt to improve decision-making meeting processes through the use of group facilitation and electronic meeting tools. The provision of staff leadership to assist volunteer Boards with their inner workings is a common task for non-profit organizations. The techniques described in this paper should be generalizable for managers in many group decision-making settings.

This paper describes how the two authors, one a facilitator and the other a staff member, systematically and progressively used different structured approaches in order to maximize overall meeting outcomes. We will take you on our journey from traditional meetings to facilitated discussions, through our use of computer-assisted on-site discussions and independent at-home use of computer survey techniques for enhancing meeting discussions, and finally, through our exploration of remote or distance-based computer-assisted meetings. We start with background information on our internal AARP client.

Background Information

The Client

The AARP Andrus Foundation, AARP's continuing memorial to its founder Dr. Ethel Percy Andrus, operates similarly to many non-profit foundations and is directed by a volunteer board. Seven volunteer Trustees come together twice a year to reach funding decisions

and award grants. The Andrus Board awards grants for applied research and action-demonstration projects. The Board must consider hundreds of competing proposals and allocate, in grants, scarce AARP member-contributed dollars to those program proposals that will most benefit older Americans. These decisions are difficult, since fewer than one in ten applicants receives funding. This is a funding rate more competitive than that of the National Institutes of Health, and those in the "aging" research community consider an Andrus Foundation grant highly prestigious (Kerin, Hollenbeck, Sprouse, and Kriner, 1996). There are often many fine applications that the Board cannot fund simply because all moneys have been exhausted.

Traditional Meetings

In the past, board meetings followed standard parliamentary procedures. A typical meeting went as follows: Prior to the meeting, Trustees received a written staff memorandum summarizing each grant application. Approximately half the proposals considered were recommended for funding, but available funds would permit only 10 to 20 percent of these to actually receive grants. During the meeting, Trustees brought motions to consider funding an applicant. Some discussion may or may not have followed, involving staff members as needed. The question was called, and the application voted up or down for funding. This process was repeated until all available funds were exhausted.

Facilitated Meetings

Several years ago, with AARP's adoption of Synectics-based meeting approaches (Nolan, 1987), a trained facilitator planned and facilitated the Trustee decision-making process during each Board meeting. In the facilitated session format, each Trustee nominated his or her top 10 applications in an open forum using flip-charts. Each proposal was discussed, with staff members responding to Trustee questions as required. Following the open discussion period, Trustees were asked to rank their top 10 applications, but this time it was a secret "straw vote." Votes were tallied, and the applications placed in rank order. Trustees then used parliamentary procedures—making appropriate motions and taking votes to award grants. The facilitator's role in facilitated consensus meetings has been described as that of a chauffeur. In this case, that role was to develop the process plan by which the Board was to reach decisions, and then execute that plan, a task analogous to chauffeuring them through the itinerary to a final destination.

The advantages of this facilitated discussion process were significant. Each Trustee was able to offer multiple proposals for consideration prior to any formal voting. Each proposal considered had the opportunity for more extensive discussion

among Trustees when needed, and individual proposals could now be considered in the larger context of all those being seriously considered for funding. More Trustees expressed their opinions both for and against a given proposal than was typical in past meetings. Foundation staff members were asked for, and expressed, their professional opinions about proposals under their responsibility. In addition, in many instances staff members were asked for opinions of research issues in larger contexts, such as the technical issues regarding sampling and experimental design, and philosophical issues concerning the importance of a particular project to a larger professional discipline. The Board relied upon these staff observations for many deliberations.

One downside to these discussions was that they were very time-consuming and mentally taxing for all participants. In the end, however, the final motions and votes went quickly and took place virtually without discussion, since deliberative discussion had already taken place.

Facilitated Technology-Assisted Decision-Making

With the installation of a Group Decision Center (GDC) room at AARP using Ventana GroupSystems software, we had a meeting facility and an electronic tool available to enhance Board decision-making. The Board had always operated under a written system of criteria and guidelines that stipulated the form to which grant applications must adhere for consideration. Until the availability of the GDC, however, final decision-making criteria were implicit to individual Board members.

Criteria-Based Decision-Making

Using facilitated discussion with the Board, a set of decision-making criteria was developed to be consistent with the AARP Vision statement, Foundation interest areas, a high-quality research investment, and responsiveness to AARP member needs/concerns (members are the primary Foundation donors). Staff members made four final criteria selections and proposed them to the Board, after which they were accepted with slight modifications. The role of staff members here was in planning the entire process which a professional facilitator would use to lead the Board in decision-making.

A general GDC discussion session was then held, during which individual Board members' written comments were anonymously collected, on a networked computer system using Ventana GroupSystems software, for each application. An open discussion session then followed to address issues and answer questions that may have been raised by the comments. With these comments from their colleagues and the automated scoring advantages of the GDC, Board members then rated applications against the four agreed-upon decision-making criteria. The GDC system automatically collected Board member ratings of each application and provided an almost instant statistical summary. A total rating score was generated by summing individual criterion ratings, and that sum was then used to rank order all applications. The summary scores and individual criterion ratings were available to all. A written record of the comments and the rankings was produced for the Board to consider overnight. This type of meeting has been described as a "supported" electronic meeting, since electronic techniques are supported by a facilitator.

The next morning, a facilitated discussion session was held while the Board considered the ranked applications in turn, using a spreadsheet prepared overnight from Board ratings and rankings. Discussion was now brief, and focused on those funding alternatives that were highly rated and ranked by the Board as a group. Final funding decisions were made using classical meeting procedures of motions, seconds, and calling the question.

Advantages of this type of decision-making approach are numerous. For the first time, explicit—rather than implicit—decision-making criteria were being used. A written record of all comments, and a detailed rating of each application according to the criteria, were obtained. For the first time, the Trustees could see their collective judgments prior to making final decisions, and would have landmarks for making reasoned comparisons among alternatives. This also meant that staff members had collective information with which to provide feedback to applicants without violating the confidentiality of the Board proceedings—a tangible byproduct of the facilitated electronic process.

The Board then expressed a keen interest in continuing to utilize the GDC in its decision-making. They also raised process concerns that, in all likelihood, they never would have considered before. For example, the Board was concerned about the independence of the individual criterion—they felt that as criteria were developed several factors overlapped with one another. This tension in decision-making has been identified in several contexts. Some describe it as art *vs.* science; others, as subjective *vs.* objective decision-making. In psychology, it is typically known as the "statistical/actuarial" controversy. The essence of the problem is best described as the following dilemma: can factors be combined in a systematic, objective, and observable way to reach a particular decision; or is the combination of factors best considered by experienced persons who will weigh them according to some unidentifiable mental/emotional process in order to reach a decision? For example, some psychologists argue that a mechanical compilation of tests and measures will yield a reasonable diagnosis based on statistical inference. Others argue that only a well-trained and experienced clinician can make a diagnosis by combining all observations and applying "clinical" judgment. We are not aware of any simple answer to this puzzle. There have, however, been efforts to develop more rigorous decision-making models (the interested reader is referred to work of Saaty and his colleagues on the Analytic Hierarchy Process: Saaty, 1980; Saaty and Kearns, 1985; Saaty & Vargas, 1986, 1991).

Output from the GDC software allowed us to analyze ratings and determine relations among overlapping criteria. In fact, the criteria were highly interrelated. Each criterion was correlated with the other criteria, with all r's $\geq .90$. The Board's concern had been an astute one—they were using only one overall criterion to rate applications. Based on this analysis the Board dropped the multiple criteria approach to decision-making and instead adopted a decision-making model whereby each Trustee would consider all of the proposals and make a global overall rating of a proposal's merit.

The At-Home Computer Survey

For the past year and a half we have used a Ventana GroupSystems optional program, GroupSystems Survey (1996), to write an electronic survey asking Board members to comment on and rate each application on their home computers. What they see is essentially what they saw before in the GDC, but now each application has become a "survey" item to be rated individually rather than one of a list of items to be rated. Comments could be entered on individual applications as desired. Staff members collect Board diskettes, e-mails, or FAXed responses for input into GroupSystems software. These surveys are completed before the meeting so that the list of any comments and the initial ratings and rankings are available for Board review prior to meetings. Now, the Board members come to the meeting prepared to discuss the initial spreadsheet ranking of applications, and they focus their attention on the merits of highly ranked applications. This technique allows us to save several hours of meeting time that had been required to get to the point in the traditional meeting in which we had used initial group rankings. This process also focuses the discussion on those applications that the group collectively considers important. Again, this type of meeting takes advantage of a facilitator to support the electronic tools.

Future Advances—Video Distance Meetings

One advantage of GDC technology, as discussed so far, is that its speed has stretched the meeting time available for the consideration of content materials— the real purpose of the meeting. Board and staff members have been intrigued by these time savings and continue to offer ideas and explore ways the decision-making process might be enhanced. We are considering the possibility of establishing an online connection, similar to a bulletin-board operation, through which Board members could call and transfer their materials electronically over the Internet.

A second approach we are considering has been described as the electronic "same time/different place" interactive meeting. The thinking here is to link the GDC with video input to individual work stations located anywhere in the country where Board members might live. This would allow us to hold decision-making meetings with distant participants who relate to each other through visual, auditory and electronic channels. Another way to think of this is as a video-conferenced call with all of the GDC computer tools available to facilitate the meeting. The electronic communication of information belongs to all group members and would necessarily predominate (some group members are at other locations and not in the meeting room), even as the meeting remains fully "supported" by a facilitator.

Summary

We have shared our journey from low-tech traditional meetings, through facilitated meetings, to the use of several iterations of group approaches supported by electronic tools and human facilitation. Finally, we have discussed several future possibilities using emerging technology to produce video distance meetings. In the end, however, the meeting process is only one factor that keeps those attending alert. Habash (1999) has extended our understanding of the complexities of using GDC-type electronic tools to support different types of distance meetings. However, we still understand little about the dynamics of distance meetings that are electronically based with regard to decision-making in real-life business contexts. Until that happens, we continue to explore the relation of new technologies and traditional meeting management issues.

References

Habash, T.C. (1999). The impact of audio- or video-conferencing and group decision tools on group perception and satisfaction in distributed meetings. *The Psychologist-Manager Journal, 3,* 211-230.

Kerin, P.B., Hollenbeck, A.R., Sprouse, B.M., & Kriner, R.E. (1996). Impact of AARP Andrus foundation grant-making in aging on professional and institutional development. *Journal of Applied Gerontology, 15,* 255-266.

Nolan, V. (1987). *The innovator's handbook—The skills of innovative management: problem solving, communication and teamwork.* London: Sphere Books Limited.

Saaty, T. (1980). *The analytic hierarchy process: Planning, priority and resource allocation.* New York: McGraw-Hill.

Saaty, T. & Kearns, K. (1985). *Analytical planning: The organization of systems.* Pittsburgh: RWS Publications.

Saaty, T. & Vargas, L. (1986). Exploring optimization through hierarchies and ratio scales. *Socioeconomic Planning in Science, 20,* 335-360.

Saaty, T. & Vargas, L. (1991). *The logic of priorities.* Pittsburgh: RWS Publications.

---

[1]Portions of this paper were presented at the annual meeting of the International Association of Facilitators, Dallas, Texas, 1996. The views presented here are those of the authors and do not necessarily represent the policies or viewpoints of AARP.

[2]*Correspondence to:*
Albert R. Hollenbeck, Ph.D.
AARP Research Group
601 E Street, N.W.
Washington, D.C. 20049
E-mail: ahollenbeck@aarp.org

THE GALLUP SCHOOL OF MANAGEMENT

GALLUP LEADERSHIP INSTITUTE
HIGH IMPACT MANAGEMENT

At The Gallup School of Management, you'll discover how the world's best managers are able to release the potential of every employee. You'll learn how to measure your company's strength – and how to make it stronger. You'll know the steps to take to ensure your organization's future. And you'll leave each seminar with opportunities for lifelong personal and professional development.

These are the proven outcomes of The Gallup School of Management's executive seminars. You and your organization can expect to achieve these results because each course is based on decades of in-depth research by The Gallup Organization, providing the most objective and unbiased data of its kind.

There's an Art to the Science of Management, and We Have the Data to Prove It

Gallup's unique Management Database, which forms the basis of all Gallup courses, is accessible to you as a Gallup School of Management alumnus.

- Over one billion answers gathered in 60 years of studying human attitudes and behavior
- Thirty years of research studying human behavior in the workplace
- Data on over 350,000 top executives, managers, and salespeople in the Gallup Workplace Management Analysis Database
- 40,000 in-depth, full-profile analyses of executive behavioral and performance measurement

---

Expect the Exceptional

Individuals attending the Gallup School of Management receive opportunities and benefits unavailable in traditional management training programs:

• Research-Based Training

The School provides a curriculum based on an in-depth profile database of over 350,000 top executive managers and salespeople that utilizes systematic, scientific research to reveal the factors that contribute to excellence. In addition, Gallup has asked over 1,000,000,000 questions on their workplaces.

• A Focus on What People Do Well

Gallup identifies individual talents and teaches participants how to lead successfully from their strengths. Awareness of these talents helps maximize performance, guides managers in selecting the right person for the right job, and encourages excellence in every individual, every day.

• Individual Learning Based on Customized Data

Gallup Consultants utilize their research skills to conduct interviews and to prepare data related to each attendee's workplace. These reports, featuring a 360° Feedback Survey that includes data from supervisors, direct reports, and peers, provide each seminar participant with personalized information and a foundation for individual action plans.

FOR MORE INFORMATION ABOUT
THE GALLUP SCHOOL OF MANAGEMENT,
CONTACT SANDE DIRKS,
EXECUTIVE DIRECTOR
1-800-288-8592, EXT. 316

THE GALLUP ORGANIZATION
PRINCETON

The Psychologist-Manager Journal
1999, Vol. 3, No. 2, 197-203

Technology and Organizations:
Internet Impacts on Managers and Management

E. Jeffrey Conklin[1]
GDSS, Inc.

This paper reviews five articles in *The Psychologist-Manager Journal* on "Technology and Its Impact on the Psychologist-Manager" (Hollenbeck, 1999a). It then introduces the concept of "virtuality" and notes how coming technological change will impact the lives and work roles of psychologist-managers.

In the past decade technological developments such as e-mail, voice mail, and the Internet have had a profound impact on organizations and on society. Indeed, a whole new genre of technology, a hybrid of computers and communication systems called information and communication technology (ICT), is changing the way we work, spend money, plan travel and conduct research, among other changes. At the heart of this paradigm shift is the universal connectivity of the Internet, a techno-societal development as momentous as the printing press and the telephone.

The size of these changes is rivaled only by the unprecedented pace at which they are occurring, especially in "knowledge organizations" (Drucker, 1994). With these changes come new opportunities and new risks. For example, in the space of less than two years, the emergence of "e-commerce" Web sites such as the bookseller Amazon.com has caused a frantic rethinking of the very nature of business, marketing, and customer satisfaction and retention. E-business is growing at a phenomenal rate, 37% per year for some services (Kraus, 1999), and this rate is expected to increase. If, as is well

known, change causes stress (e.g., McWhinney, 1997) more must be learned about the level of organizational stress managers face, as the very rules of business are being reinvented by a global electronic economy.

The five papers in this section explore some of these issues from a wide variety of perspectives. Greenberg (1999) reviews the impacts of ICT on traditional applications of psychology, such as personnel assessment and selection and organizational development. Civiello (1999) discusses the unique position of psychologist-managers in addressing the security risks posed by the rapid movement of most organizations into cyberspace. Habash (1999) reports on empirical studies of technologies used for "virtual teams"—work groups that are geographically dispersed and are thus heavily dependent on ICT for their ability to successfully collaborate. Hollenbeck (1999) reports on the impacts and innovations in research occasioned by his membership associations' efforts to better serve its members over the Internet.

Three broad themes emerge from these papers. The first is the deep impact of ICT on groups, organizations, and society. Managers may not use the Internet directly, but they cannot isolate themselves from the subtle and ubiquitous effects these ICT's are having on their organization. For example, the "democratization" of the workplace, a movement that has been afoot for many years, has surely been accelerated by the ability of any worker to immediately communicate with top management via e-mail. That kind of access does not have to be exercised often to begin, perhaps subtly, to change power relations throughout the organization. While it is commonly known that the availability of fax machines contributed to the student revolution of Chinese students in Tienanmen Square (Rodan, 1996), how well are the impacts of e-mail and chat rooms on our own staff members understood? There are new opportunities, such as for improved service (Greenberg, 1999) and improved information about customers and members (Hollenbeck, 1999b). But there are also increased risks, such as the easy loss of proprietary information through indiscriminant sharing of such information by a "trusted insider" (Civiello, 1999).

The second theme is the rapid acceleration of the pace of change. The ever-escalating increase in technological innovation requires that we understand how the consequent rapid organizational change affects organizations and the managerial role, and that we learn and teach mechanisms for coping with the often destabilizing shifts in identity and relationships.

The third theme is the development of "virtuality" in organizational life. Teams and work groups need no longer be geographically close. As these virtual teams increasingly conduct virtual meetings on the Internet, it is necessary to better understand the impact of the loss of direct face-to-face contact. Certain business processes, such as making policy or resource allocation decisions, are difficult enough to accomplish face to face. We need to better understand the psychology of creating shared understanding and commitment when key players start to conduct more and more of their interactions through conference calls or e-mail connections.

Brief Reviews of the Papers

Although he does not mention the term "information and communication technology," Greenberg (1999) asserts that the information and communication technology worlds are integrating, and that the Internet will soon equal or exceed the telephone as the medium of choice for business communications. Greenberg points out that traditional research sources were not as useful in preparing to write his paper as was talking to colleagues and networking, a theme echoed by other writers. He cites John Naisbitt's phrase "high tech-high touch" to illustrate that the surge of technology development, often cold and impersonal, has heightened our need for human contact and community, and thus is causing "a shift to a more person-centered approach to organizational psychology." Not only is that technology creating new ways to perform traditional managerial functions in the organization, it is also providing new methods for recognizing and intervening with the human side of management.

Greenberg reviews recent technological developments in three areas: employment processing, testing and assessment, and organizational development. The array of ICT's being used in these areas include PC-based and web-based tools, multimedia software, the telephone, video-conferencing, and Interactive Voice

Response (IVR) systems. Many of the new technologies come with new opportunities, such as democratization of information, faster and more customized delivery of services, and more effective inclusion of remote participants and organizations. These opportunities are attended by new risks, such as the challenge of validating assessments and tests that are being offered over the Web, and concerns about the security of sensitive psychological data.

While the news is mostly good, Greenberg points out that there are some areas in which the very openness and flexibility of the Internet makes it a poor match for some traditional functions, such as testing. Until there are better mechanisms for establishing identity and maintaining security on the Internet, its use in valid personnel testing will be limited.

Civiello (1999) examines the security risks inherent in the openness of the ICT revolution, exploring computer crime, economic and industrial espionage, and ways that managers can help to mitigate organizational exposure. The central concern of the paper is that "trusted insiders," employees who have access to proprietary information, are increasingly at risk of betraying their organizations' best interests in cyberspace. Two factors struck me as particularly compelling with regard to this issue. First, Civiello explores the impact on the psychology of self when an increasing percentage of a person's time is spent in an increasingly vivid virtual environment, where traditional concepts of reality change. Cybersex is one example of how real the perception of intimacy can be in the absence of face-to-face and social context cues.

A second factor identified by Civiello is the sense of community often present in cyberspace, which can lead to allegiances that can actually be stronger than those within the workplace community. An example of this phenomenon is the situation in which a programmer distributes a company-proprietary piece of software to a fellow programmer at a competing company, because the ethic of open sharing of information is particularly strong in the academic and technical communities. Here we see a fundamental tension between the emerging culture of openness and flexibility of the Internet and the core values of organizations and nations that draw a sharp line between "insider" and "outsider." The values that increase the security risk posed by people who grew up in a world in which some of their best friends are people they have never met in countries they have never visited may be the very values that give those people strong identities as global, rather than ethnocentric, citizens.

In his empirical study of technology and work groups, Habash (1999) reports on the impact of group decision support tools on "virtual teams"—work groups that do not work face to face and are thus dependent on ICT for their ability to successfully collaborate. This paper joins a long history of research and debate on how—and whether—different technologies can support virtual teamwork. The simplest and most familiar technology for virtual teamwork is the conference call, also known as audio-conferencing, in which members of a small or large group share a telephone call. Habash (1999) cites studies showing that the quality of the audio is a critical factor in the usefulness of the conference call.

There are limits to the kinds of work such groups can accomplish with audio-conferencing only, but the research on the incremental impact of video-conferencing is equivocal. As Habash notes, the effects of adding a video connection range from slightly negative to strongly positive. The Habash paper reports on his study of the incremental impact of a third dimension in the mix: group decision support tools (GDST). GDST, typically used in a specially equipped meeting room in which the each meeting participant has a networked computer, includes tools for electronically brainstorming ideas and voting on or ranking them. After exploring the use of GDST with virtual teams, Habash suggests that such technology may allow geographically distant participants to do better the things they would do if they were face to face. This suggests a marvelous departure from the usual technocentric approach of testing the impacts of new technologies on users, which is akin to looking for your keys under the streetlight because that is where the light is best. What if geographically dispersed teams, equipped with the right mix of tools and practices, could actually outperform face-to-face groups at certain tasks?

In brief, Habash (1999) found that video-conferencing without GDST improved perceptions of social presence and communication interface over audioconferencing, but that adding GDST to video-conferencing did not result in any additional improvement. However, GDST alone also improved these same measures. This is evidence that any kind of shared display, whether video pictures of the other participants or computer screens depicting their ideas, improves a virtual meeting. This is consistent with years of research showing the power of shared display for the success of collaborative work, whether face-to-face or virtual (Schrage, 1990). One problem with this study is that GDST is more obscure than audio- and video-conferencing, and is generally applied in a face-to-face situation, so the problems with GDST may simply reflect lack of familiarity, or the fact that the tools themselves are more tailored to face-to-face meeting environments.

Hollenbeck (1999b) reports on the surprising innovations in research approaches occasioned by his membership associations' efforts to better serve their members on the web. Hollenbeck observes that change is occurring too fast to study with traditional research methods, but could also have noted that there are now emerging "virtual journals" that accept electronic papers, conduct the review and referee process on the Internet, and publish research papers "in Internet time" on the web, sometimes with the reviewer's commentary hyperlinked to the original paper. Like Greenberg, Hollenbeck found that the social network, not the library, is currently the best source of information about Internet research.

Hollenbeck described many complications in adapting web-based tools to research. He aptly notes the web system actually tracks too much data, in too much detail, rather like trying to follow an animal's tracks in the dirt using a microscope. The ultimate solution for the immediate problems was statistics; using sampling and a theory about visitor behavior, they were able to make some sense of the immense volume of data. Hollenbeck also describes a framework for long-term research that illuminates three major approaches to understanding the Internet and its impact on organizations and society. The "actors" approach is intriguing because it assumes that reality is a construct of actors, and that it is created (rather than simply described) through the dialogue among the actors.

Finally, Cryer and Hollenbeck (1999) report on one group's use of facilitation and electronic meeting tools. Their case study illustrates the benefits of electronic decision support tools, as well as the natural evolution of a group's sophistication in the use of such tools. The task described was essentially a resource allocation process, such as budgeting, which is almost always difficult to do well. The decision criteria are often difficult to articulate and align on, and often the stakes are high.

Cryer and Hollenbeck (1999) show that with good facilitation, group decision technologies can help a group work better and faster. The paper describes some specific facilitation techniques that can be used in other, similar situations. For example, the technology can help with "time shifting" some of the work to pre-meeting preparation, so that some tasks are completed before the meeting ever starts, allowing the group to make better use of its collective time when assembled for the meeting.

However, it should also be noted that the specific resource allocation task that Cryer and Hollenbeck describe—awarding grants based on applications—is in many ways easier than similar tasks that managers must routinely perform. The players who come to the resource allocation table are much more personally and politically involved with the decision outcomes than the group described in the case. Managers often have a strong sense of connection or identification with some of the projects and departments whose budget is being decided, and no connection at all with others. Often there is some level of internal conflict, as well as hidden agendas, back-room negotiations, and political maneuvering involved in the process of allocating scarce organizational resources.

To facilitate such meetings effectively is a great challenge. For example, it is often not possible for the participants to agree on a clear set of decision criteria or on their ranking. These meetings may require a face-to-face presence simply because the communication process is very delicate, and all nuances are potentially significant. The decision support tools that facilitators choose for such situations may include group brainstorming and voting tools, but must also go beyond these. They must create an environment, whether electronically or manually, that keeps the participants focused on the issues and information at hand, and gives them a clear shared display of the status of their discussions and decisions. Such tools exist (for example, QuestMap™— see *http://www.softbicycle.com*), but they require significant training and practice in order to be used effectively.

Some Thoughts on Virtuality

You can tell a lot about a culture from its use of language. It is now ostensibly possible to create a new way of doing business buy simply putting the letter "e" in front of an existing one: e-banking, e-travel, e-commerce. Similarly, our culture has made heavy use of the term "virtual," meaning a process which takes place within cyberspace that mimics or mirrors an existing familiar process. Thus, a "virtual meeting" is one in which participants communicate electronically, either at the same time but from different locations, or at different points in time, or both. It is now possible, though not yet common, for virtual employees in a virtual company to hold virtual meetings to discuss new virtual products.

A clear benefit of virtuality is freedom from the constraints of time and space. Just as the VCR allows one to "time shift" a favorite program into a time slot that is more convenient, so e-mail, bulletin boards, and other computer collaboration tools allow members of a work group to participate in a "virtual conversation" as they have slices of time available. Similarly, location does not matter so much any more. At the time of this writing there are brisk sales of a new device that allows the user to send and receive e-mail by radio at the push of a button with no wires to connect or calls to place. Similarly, I have acquaintances who use a satellite system to maintain regular e-mail contact with their friends and family from whatever ocean they happen to be sailing on—easily and fairly cheaply.

As promising as this revolution sounds, it still leaves people out. There are those who have tried telecommuting and have returned to fighting rush-hour traffic. Some just need the solidity of direct human contact. Similarly, many of those who have been required to participate on a virtual team or project have had bad experiences. It is hard enough to collaborate on a complex project with tight timelines. When the players are in different locations, you further complicate the process with scheduling and time zone differences, lack of face-to-face contact with colleagues, and immature technologies. As a result, stress and the likelihood of project failure increase.

In recent years, one thing has become clear: a key element in the success of a virtual project is the strength of the group's "shared display." If a work group has a face-to-face meeting, chances are they pass documents around the table and make notes or pictures on a flip-chart or white board in the room. The passed-around documents and the white board are their shared display. Even hand gestures made as someone is speaking are part of their shared display. However, when a virtual work group meets, by conference call or video-conference, they do not have the same richness of shared display. It is easy

for misunderstandings to take place, and harder to detect and repair them.

It is perhaps difficult to appreciate the power of shared display—and the impact of its absence—unless one has tried to work on a significant project with others using only the telephone and an Internet connection. An example might serve to clarify the issue.

Recently I was working with a colleague on the design of a training curriculum. We had a meeting scheduled to review the text-based draft she had been working on. Since she had been working from home that day, we had a "virtual meeting" using the phone. At first we tried to create a shared display by looking at her document together using Microsoft's NetMeeting™. This system is an "application sharing" tool which allows several people to simultaneously view (and even edit) a document on one person's computer via the Internet. Unfortunately, on this day we had technical problems with the software, so my colleague sent the document to me via e-mail. I was able to quickly open and read it, so it seemed like we had a good solution—a workable "shared display."

Then the problems started. As I read over her document I started to make suggestions about changes. I marked my changes on my copy of the document and then described them to her. She made changes to her document. After about 15 minutes of this, it became apparent that somewhere we had gotten "out of synch"—somehow the changes she had made to her document were in different places from the ones I had made. So we spent several minutes going through all the changes I had suggested, trying to get our copies of the document to correspond.

This scene is probably repeated thousands of times every day. It is a clear and simple case of an insufficient "shared display." My colleague and I were fortunate in that it only took us a few minutes to detect and repair our miscommunication. Imagine, however, a dozen people, working on a large and complex project with multiple documents, with hours spent every day in collaborative meetings. The opportunities for confusion and disorientation abound, and with them come a strain on interpersonal relationships. When people know each other well, collaborating remotely is only a moderate challenge. However if, as is increasingly the case, people who have never met face to face find themselves on the same virtual team, then the lack of an effective shared display is likely to seriously challenge their ability to collaborate, and to build stronger relationships in the process of collaborating.

Creating rich and dynamic shared displays is not simply a technical problem. What characteristics of working together in a face-to-face setting are really useful and essential? How can we successfully translate these aspects of human communication and relationship into the emerging "virtual world" of organizations conducting transactions, projects, and business over the Internet? This is an area requiring both research and practice, but one in which the psychologist-manager can play a critical role.

References

Civiello, C.L. (1999). Cyberspace, trusted insiders, and organizational threat: The role of the psychologist-manager. *The Psychologist-Manager Journal, 3,* 149-166.

Cryer, R. and Hollenbeck, A.R. (1999). Case study: Traditional facilitation skills combined with group decision technologies. *The Psychologist-Manager Journal, 3,* 191-195.

Drucker, P. F. (1994). The age of social transformation. *The Atlantic Monthly, 274, 5,* 53-80.

Greenberg, C.I. (1999). Innovations and advancements in technology for psychologists working in organizations. *The Psychologist-Manager Journal, 3,* 181-190.

Habash, T.C. (1999). The impact of audio- or video-conferencing and group decision tools on group perception and satisfaction in distributed meetings. *The Psychologist-Manager Journal, 3,* 211-230.

Hollenbeck, A.R. (1999a). Introduction to the special section on technology and its impact on the psychologist-manager. *The Psychologist-Manager Journal, 3,* 147-148.

Hollenbeck, A.R. (1999b). Using the Internet and World Wide Web (WWW): Amazing sites/amazing insights. *The Psychologist-Manager Journal, 3,* 167-179.

Kraus, S. (September, 1999). 1999 MONITOR Preview. *Yankelovich Monitor Live.99,* (Teleconference).

McWhinney, W. (1997). *Paths of change: Strategic choices for organizations and society—revised edition.* Thousand Oaks, CA: Sage.

Rodan, G. (1996). *Information technology and political control in Singapore.* Working Paper 26 of the Japan Policy Research Institute, Cardiff, CA. www.jpri.org./jpri/wp26.html.

Schrage, M. (1989). *No more teams! Mastering the dynamics of creative collaboration.* New York: Doubleday.

[1]*Correspondence to:*
Jeff Conklin, Ph.D.
Fellow, GDSS, Inc.
1000 Thomas Jefferson Street, N.W.
Washington, D.C. 20007
E-mail: jconklin@gdss.com

The Psychologist-Manager Journal
1999, Vol. 3, No. 2, 205-208

New Technologies and Old Issues:
Using Technology to Enhance the Elixir of Discovery

Joel M. Reaser[1]
AARP Information Technology Solutions

This paper provides commentary on the articles in this special section of *The Psychologist-Manager Journal* on "Technology and Its Impact on the Psychologist-Manager" (Hollenbeck, 1999a). Each of the articles in this special section is briefly discussed, with strengths and omissions identified. Technological innovation, as evidenced from this special section, is placed in the context of organizational change and discovery.

This article summarizes reactions to the special section in this issue on "Technology and Its Impact on the Psychologist-Manager." I will first comment briefly on each of the articles in the special section, and then make a few overarching remarks.

Each of these articles addresses a different aspect of technology and management.

Eighty percent of computer hacking activity is carried out by those who are, or who were at one time, affiliated with the organization whose computers are being hacked (Nordwell, 1997). In response to this and other types of intentional cyber-threats, Civiello (1999) suggests that the organizational psychologist has a significant role to play. The emphasis in the article is on the means to assess potential illegal and undesirable behavior. Civiello provides an extensive discussion of the ways in which disgruntled or unethical employees, and current or former employees, can compromise corporate information and systems: theft or misuse of trade secrets or sensitive personnel information; exploitation of other employees; misallocation of time; misrepresentation of self or the organization.

The project described in Hollenbeck's article (1999b) is a good example of the challenges and opportunities presented to organizational researchers by the technologies now available. The Web is both the object of research and a part of the methodology of applied organizational and market research. Hollenbeck shares the pragmatic details of his team's attempts, and final successes, in profiling the visitors to AARP's "Webplace," and a parallel effort to assess the usability (ease of navigation) of the site. In both cases, what appeared simple was not.

Carl Greenberg (1999) reviewed a number of recent technological innovations that are available, and suggested many ways in which they directly affect the nature and content of managers' lives. The Web, networked PCs, and the applications and accessories that have evolved with them have changed the workplace and changed the ways in which we acquire research data from those in the workplace. As Greenberg notes, the Web is quickly becoming a primary research tool. It has, for example, revolutionized the job search/candidate recruitment process. Networked computers now make "360-degree" evaluations administratively and computationally possible in short time frames. Similarly, computer-based task simulations provide an excellent skill assessment process for certain kinds of jobs.

Greenberg also identified issues created by the availability of these technologies. For example, just about anyone can assemble an "assessment instrument" that appears on the surface to be practically useful, but often there is no basis for determining the validity or reliability of such an instrument. Data security and individual anonymity or confidentiality are important issues which must be addressed in all Web-based research. Although Greenberg does not address other technological impacts (e.g., collaborative decision-making tools and supervision-at-a-distance), and would benefit from more specific examples of organizations in which these technologies are being successfully employed, the article is still a valuable overview of some contemporary uses of technology in management.

The challenge is, how can organizations appropriately balance the need for efforts to protect themselves and to create an environment in which people feel attached to each other and to the organizational mission and purpose? Since very few people intentionally hurt the people and things they value, the larger question becomes, how much effort should we put into identifying individuals who exhibit risk factors versus the effort spent identifying ways to have the individuals in the organizations feel valued and committed?

A number of legitimate methodological concerns are addressed by Hollenbeck (1999b) within the context of Arbnor and Bjerke's (1997) framework of three approaches for creating business knowledge. The project team evolved a methodology that included aspects of each knowledge approach, and collected data relevant to each. Hollenbeck devotes the remainder of his article to reviewing Web sites. Several of these are of professional interest. Overall, the article provides useful information for the practicalities confronting those of us conducting research in our "Internet-speed" organizational settings.

The case study by Cryer and Hollenbeck (1999) provides a useful perspective on how creative persons use new technologies to address longstanding issues. The case illustrates the natural history of the introduction of new processes, as the authors attempted to apply group decision-making technologies to assist a board in making funding decisions about grant applications. In this example, technology saved time and streamlined the decision process, but the improved process did not appear to change the underlying decision-making process the Board had been using all along.

Finally, Habash (1999) notes that technological advances have made it possible for meetings to take place almost anywhere or anytime. Video, including web-based video, and computer network-based (again including web-based) conferencing services have helped to create dramatically different meeting environments. Habash presents evidence of rigorous applied research, and helps extend the understanding of the human experience of meetings held at a distance, so that these meetings may be as productive and fulfilling as face-to-face meetings.

Habash examines the impact of using two-way video and group-decision support tools to augment two-way audio (i.e., telephone conference calls) to conduct meetings at a distance. The results of the research demonstrate that video can make a difference in the perception of meeting participants on some measures, but that the use of group tools does not. The really important aspect of this study is that it was conducted in a large organization, with people working on real organizational problems. An organization's use of technology for meeting and decision-support often depends more on organizational culture and resources than on research findings. However, it is clear that these emerging technologies will be a major determinant of when, where, and how we meet in the future. We need to continue to develop those technologies in a way that is not only productive, but rewarding as a human experience, and to further research empirically what works and what does not.

Technology and Human Purpose: The Elixir of Discovery in Organizations

One of the most important implications of the technologies discussed in this special section is that those who influence organizational policy and behavior (organizational behaviorists, psychologist-managers, board members, staff and others) have an opportunity to invest in *discovery behaviors* on behalf of our organizations and their employees. This investment should extend beyond the traditional concepts of research and beyond the focus on quarterly profits. Managers need to understand that discovery is not an ephemeral fad, or even just the driving force of the 1990's stock market. It is the elixir that allows organizations to continuously refresh their employees, and the systems and procedures by which they service their clients.

In fact, people love to discover new ways of doing things. Sometimes they are simply tired of the existing way. More often, there is some purpose to the quest. Whether the purpose is to save a few steps or to make millions of dollars, people are driven by the needs that give rise to individual and collective inventiveness. Technology has not changed this need; in fact, it is the product of this need.

One example of an approach to investing in discovery occurred in 1991 at AARP. A new department was created in the Research Group, the formal title of which was Statistics, Methods and Research Technology (it was called the SMaRT Department). The department's mission was discovery—to find new methodologies and technologies to make better research, to identify better ways to analyze and understand data, to create better ways to disseminate results, to improve communications with clients through technology and to enhance and support organizational decision-making. The SMaRT Department quickly developed a discovery mentality that bred creativity, supportive competition, and positive client impact. Within four years, the department had implemented a Windows environment for research staff, GIS (geographic information systems) as an analytical and presentation methodology; a meeting room with meetings-at-a-distance technologies; automated survey scanning; voice response technology; computer presentation technologies; and the creation of the AARP Webplace and its organizational presence on the Internet.

The listing of new technologies was only one aspect of the discovery. More importantly, the acts of discovery created new energy in the staff. For example:
• weekly   informal   "Technology

Tuesdays" information-sharing sessions were created for, and by, staff;

• members of the traditional computer department sought employment in the new department;

• staff at all levels sought training in a wide variety of technological tools to build personal skills and knowledge, and to promote the activities of the research projects on which they worked.

Organizational professionals are uniquely positioned to promote formal and informal activities that facilitate discovery within their organizations. Staff members follow this leadership when they are part of the discovery process. Electronic technologies are simply the most recent version of tools that we have always used in our organizations to better fulfill our human purposes. As Margaret Wheatley and Myron Keller-Rogers (1996, p. 3) put it in *A Simpler Way*: "People are intelligent, creative, adaptive, self-organizing, and meaning-seeking. Organizations are living systems. They too are intelligent, creative, adaptive, self-organizing, and meaning-seeking." Our job as psychologist-managers and organizational citizens is to continuously nurture the discovery elixir.

References

Civiello, C.L. (1999). Cyberspace, trusted insiders, and organizational threat: The role of the psychologist manager. *The Psychologist-Manager Journal, 3,* 149-166.

Cryer, R. and Hollenbeck, A.R. (1999). Case study: Traditional facilitation skills combined with group decision technologies. *The Psychologist-Manager Journal, 3,* 191-195.

Greenberg, C.I. (1999). Innovations and advancements in technology for psychologists working in organizations. *The Psychologist-Manager Journal, 3,* 167-176.

Habash, T.C. (1999). The impact of audio- or video-conferencing and group decision tools on group perception and satisfaction in distributed meetings. *The Psychologist-Manager Journal, 3,* 211-230.

Hollenbeck, A.R. (1999a). Introduction to the special section on technology and its impact on the psychologist-manager. *The Psychologist-Manager Journal, 3,* 147-148.

Hollenbeck, A.R. (1999b). Using the Internet and World Wide Web (WWW): Amazing sites/amazing insights. *The Psychologist-Manager Journal, 3,* 167-179.

Nordwell, B.D. (1997, June). Cyber-threats place infrastructure at risk. *Aviation Week and Space Technology, 146,* 51.

Wheatley, M., & Keller-Rogers, M. (1996). *A Simpler Way.* San Francisco: Berrett-Koehler Publishers.

---

[1]*Correspondence to:*
Joel M. Reaser, Ph.D.
Information Technology Strategy, Planning and Learning
AARP Information Technology Solutions
601 E Street, N.W.
Washington, D.C 20049
E-mail: jreaser@aarp.org.

[2]The views presented here are those of the author and do not necessarily represent the policies or viewpoints of AARP.

Section III:

RESEARCH: TOOLS FOR THE PSYCHOLOGIST-MANAGER

The Psychologist-Manager Journal
1999, Vol. 3, No. 2, 211-230

The Impact of Audio- or Video-Conferencing and Group Decision Tools on Group Perception and Satisfaction in Distributed Meetings

Tony F. Habash[1, 2, 3]

AARP

This study investigated the impact of communication media (audio-conferencing [AC] *vs.* video-conferencing [VC]) and the use/non-use of group decision support tools (GDST) on group perception and goal satisfaction in synchronous distributed group decision tasks. A factorial design with repeated measures on the communication medium factor was employed. Professionals (*n*=72) from a large non-profit organization solved real-world tasks in small groups. Perception of social presence, of communication interface, and of communication effectiveness was assessed. Individual personal satisfaction with the meeting process and outcome, and perception of the final decision quality were also measured. The study found that organizations can get all the benefits of using GDST in distributed meetings without losing much in terms of perception of communication interface. If GDST are used, audio-conferencing (AC) is sufficient, since adding video-conferencing (VC) provided little or no additional benefit. Implications for managers are discussed.

A face-to-face gathering is perceived to be the most socially rich meeting environment. However, organizations do not always have the luxury of face-to-face meetings. Hence, the need to build distributed meeting environments (where groups can meet in different geographical locations at the same time or at different times) through the use of information systems and communication technologies. The new environment created by different kinds of communication media as well as group decision support tools can impact participants' perceptions and social interactions, and the quality of the decisions reached. Also, the meeting process itself can be highly affected by the type of technology used. This study focuses on the distributed meeting environment

using a combination of communication media, two-way full-duplex (both parties can participate at the same time) audio-and/or video-conferencing capabilities, and group decision support tools (GDST). The study combined meeting facilitation (usually same-time/same-place), using group decision support tools (GDST), with conferencing technologies to add another dimension to the same-time/different-place setting.

The promise of GDST arose from the continuous need for meetings in organizations. While the reasons for such meetings might vary, people need to meet to get work done, and chances are they will continue to do so. The question is how to make such meetings more productive. To this end, numerous efforts in the last two decades have been channeled around finding methods, systems, and techniques to improve the efficiency and effectiveness of meetings (Nunamaker, Briggs, & Romano, 1995a). These efforts led to the creation of electronic meeting systems (EMS) (Nunamaker et al., 1995a). Since then, various labels and acronyms have been used in the literature and by commercial manufacturers to refer to such systems. These include meetingware (Di Pietro, 1995), group decision support systems (GDSS) (Turoff, Hiltz, Bahgat, & Rana, December 1993), and computer-mediated meetings. In this study we will refer to such systems as group decision support tools (GDST).

Distributed group support systems are expected to be widely used in the near future as the means to enable dispersed but connected workgroups or teams to work together (Boland, Maheshwarl, Te'eni, Schwartz, & Tenaski, 1992; Buckley & Yen, 1990; Turoff et al., December 1993). The need for a distributed environment, however, requires that GDST be integrated with other conferencing and communication capabilities to allow for a distributed synchronous meeting to take place.

Bringing together all these technologies and solutions to build an environment for non-face-to-face decision meetings is not a trivial endeavor, since many variables could affect the outcome, the process, and the group perception. One of the challenges is to bring together the right mix of technology and tools to optimize such meetings.

GDST research usually brings people together in "decision rooms" (Turoff et al., December 1993) and observes the meetings. A meeting incorporates many elements that contribute to its dynamics. These range from the people processes to the physical environment, and are affect-ed by the type of meeting, the group size, and individual and group motivations (Nunamaker et al., 1995a).

Over the last 10 to 15 years, interdisciplinary research into the potential impact of GDST on meetings has been conducted (Cass, Heintz, & Kaiser, 1992; Dennis, George, Jessup, Nunamaker, & Vogel, 1988). However, interpersonal communications in the GDST context are not yet well understood (Nour & Yen, 1992). The last three decades have also witnessed an exponential increase in the amount of research on the impact of conferencing technologies, mainly on audio- and video-mediated conferencing, participants' perceptions, and meeting outcomes and processes (Cass et al., 1992; Finn, 1997; Harmon, Schneer, & Hoffman, February 1995).

With few exceptions, there has been little progress in integrating GDST with conferencing technologies to create a multi media-enhanced distributed decision-making environment. The concept here is to use GDST to structure interactions among group members in different places by combining GDST with audio- and video-conferencing technologies (see, e.g., Chidambaram & Jones, 1993; Dennis et al., 1988; Johansen et al., 1991; Pinsonneault & Kraemer, 1990), thus adding the dimension of person-to-person interaction and dialogue to distributed meetings.

Both "groupware" (GDST) and "computer-supported collaborative work" (CSCW) are umbrella terms that have been used previously to describe many of the applications and tools that are designed to support groups in doing their work. Among these applications are group support systems, video teleconferencing, group conferencing, electronic brainstorming, electronic conferencing, and electronic meeting systems.

EMS, as defined by Nunamaker, Dennis, Valacich, Vogel, & George, (1991), is typically based on a network of personal computers, usually one for each participant. Participants use the computers to support their meetings through a set of tools that structure the meeting process. These tools facilitate a range of processes, from electronic brainstorming and electronic idea organization to electronic voting and electronic ranking. Typically, the meeting happens in a special room if it is face-to-face, or participants could be in distributed geographical locations with access to the EMS tools through a computer network of some sort.

Nunamaker, Vogel, Heminger, and Martz (June 1989) reported higher process and outcome effectiveness, efficiency and user satisfaction among groups using GDST than among groups using no automated support tools. They also reported a 56% time savings associated with the use of GDST. Pinsonneault and Kraemer (1990) reported that an increase in participants' satisfaction with the final decision and the decision process followed when GDST was used. Similar results were reported by Di Pietro (1995), including improved decision quality, improved buy-in with the decision, an increase in the number of ideas generated in the meeting, and increased participation. GDST removes hierarchical barriers, such as status symbols, and encourages feedback. He concluded that a balance between the use of GDST and classic discussion methods positively influences the participants' perceptions of the meeting quality, and their personal satisfaction.

Not all findings have been positive. Gray, Vogel, & Beauclair (1990), have reviewed most of the studies that address the impact of GDST on group performance. These studies examine the quality of the final decision and the number of alternatives generated in the meeting. While several of these studies report that GDST has a positive impact on group performance, others conclude that GDST has no impact. In rare instances, studies have documented negative perceptions of group members regarding the impact of GDST on group performance (Watson, 1987).

In summary, the research findings as they relate to the use of GDST to support face-to-face meetings report mostly positive results regarding the impact of GDST on the meeting process and outcome, and on participants' perceptions. The same studies report the conditions necessary for such success, including preplanning of the meeting, a skilled facilitator, and the capability of the group to adapt to the use of the tools over time. Note that the nature of work performed by groups in different locations at the same time differs from that of groups working face to face. Thus, any investigation of the distributed synchronous meeting environment should not necessarily be limited to dynamics deriving from our understanding of face-to-face meetings only. Distributed meetings may have their own elements and variables that impact their chances for success which, if properly understood, might lead to the development of communicative practices different from those that make face-to-face meetings successful (Dourish, Adler, Bellottio, & Henderson, 1996).

Audio-conferencing. The first telephone call was brought about by the need to bring people together in a distributed setting. Indeed, several studies have concluded that high-quality audio is a critical element in distributed synchronous meetings, whether or not video is used (Fish, Kraut, & Chalfonte, 1990; Maaranen, 1995; Pagani & Mackay, 1993; Tang &

Issacs, 1992). Audio-conferencing allows for the flexible management of collaboration and interaction through the monitoring of activities on an ongoing basis, and for assessing the availability and engagement of participants. Harmon et al., (February 1995) reported that well-established decision teams are likely to produce the same results whether they meet face to face or by audio-conferencing.

Video-conferencing. From a technological perspective, video-conferencing can include video-phone, desktop video-conferencing, mobile video-conferencing systems, and specially dedicated video-conferencing facilities. The communication media that link participants together using video-conferencing can range from telephone lines to the Internet. Different technological combinations affect audio and video quality, the costs of using and building such solutions, and the requirements to operate and maintain systems. All these elements could be factors that impact user perceptions of such technology.

Audio- vs. video-conferencing. Findings on the impact of video versus audio alone in a teleconferencing session have been mixed. Chapanis, Ochsman, Parrish, & Weeks (1972) found that audio was the determining element that impacted performance, and that video had no significant effects on behavior. Gale (1989) found no differences in the quality of the output due to the use of video.

Anderson et al., (1997) report little benefit from seeing one's partner in a collaborative problem-solving task. Others suggest that video-conferencing is of benefit for more "social" tasks, such as negotiation or bargaining. Heath and Luff (1991, 1992) report that video-conferencing interferes with the techniques by which talk is regulated and managed in face-to-face communication. This supports the conclusion of Anderson et al. (1997) that video-conferencing does not deliver all the advantages of face-to-face interactions. These researchers describe the importance of video fidelity on perception and outcome. Low-bandwidth video-conferencing, where audio and video signals are delayed, clearly has a harmful effect, impairing task outcomes and smooth communication.

In contrast, some studies found added value from the use of video-conferencing compared with audio-conferencing alone. They also compared video-conferencing with face-to-face interaction. It was found that with video-conferencing, more speech was used to achieve the same level of performance than when audio-conferencing alone was used, indicating that the video component encourages interaction among participants (Anderson et al., 1997). This might be due to the heightened sense of social presence that frequent gazing produces in video-conferencing. The authors thus concluded that video-conferencing is useful for task efficiency, even when social factors are not a central component of the task. Other research found that the availability of a video channel had a positive impact on outcome, performance, and group perception (Olson, Olson, & Meader, 1995; Rutter, Stephanson, & Dewey, 1981).

It is worth noting that several studies concentrated on comparing properties of video-conferencing to everyday face-to-face interaction (Gaver, Smets, & Overbeeke, 1995; Heath & Luff, 1992). Olson & Olson (1997), and Olson, Olson, & Meader, (1997) reported that with remote work there is more clarification regardless of the presence of video. The authors also reported that video does not encourage participants to be more engaged, nor to discuss things more critically. However, video-conferencing was preferred by participants over audio-conferencing, and regarded as equally preferable as face-to-face work. This finding was consistent with the work of Isaacs and Tang (1997), who reported an increase in user satisfaction due to the use of the video-conferencing. This is mainly due to the fact that video enhances the users' experience, helps with interpreting communication through visual cues, increases awareness, and establishes identity and recognition, especially when participants have never seen each other before.

Other studies tried to investigate the impact of video-conferencing over time. Dykstra-Erickson et al., (1995) reported that the use of video-conferencing communication over extended periods of time leads to increased levels of acceptability by the users, since as they adapt to the technology they shift the focus from the technology to the communication itself. They also noted the emergence of a "local visual language" over a ten-week period of using video-conferencing. Such studies illuminate the potential use of video-conferencing as a means of facilitating interaction between workgroups and teams on a daily basis. Such use might lead to communication practices and protocols that are simply different from face-to-face practices and protocols. Also, each group might end up with communication practices that are unique to the group.

Several factors could help account for a variety of results found in the research in this field. These include the architecture of the technology, the equipment used, the analytic approach, and group size and characteristics (Dennis et al., 1988). The tasks performed, the reliability of the media, the comfort level of the group members in using new technology, the quality of the audio, the video fidelity, and the collected data could all be factors

that impacted the results of these studies (Finn, 1997; Fish, Kraut, Root, & Rice, 1992; Harrison, 1992; Isaacs & Tang, 1993; O'Conaill, Whittaker, & Wilbur, 1993; Sellen, 1995). This leads to the general conclusion that personal and situational factors are significant predictors in implementation success (Lucas, 1981), and since findings in this field of literature are situation-specific, a deeper understanding of distributed group work will contribute to better system design and usage.

With the maturity of video-conferencing tools, and the widespread use of the Internet and networked computers, the use of such technology may soon become second nature in businesses and academia. Video may be the answer to creating an atmosphere and feeling of closeness in distant collaboration.

The Distributed Synchronous Meeting Environment

The key to conducting successful distributed synchronous meetings is providing the means for "place" to emerge from "space." While the need for people to meet at a distance, by means of communication and group decision support media, is very strong in today's business world, the elements of success for such environments need to be studied.

Creating an environment that fosters distributed synchronous meetings appears to require an integrated approach combining audio-conferencing and video-conferencing with GDST. There are several initiatives and studies aimed at testing the impact of an integrated distributed meeting environment on group perception and performance. Chidambaram & Jones (1993), for example, reported on a research project in which group perception and performance were tested in a distributed meeting environment using GDST and audio-conferencing, and then compared with the results from a face-to-face setting. The outcome of this study showed that the use of GDST lowered perception of social presence, as did audio-conferencing, when compared to the face-to-face situation. On the other hand, the use of GDST in the face-to-face setting did not impact communication effectiveness. The same study also found that the number of alternatives generated was higher for groups using GDST, but that the use of audio-conferencing did not produce a higher number of alternatives compared to the results in a face-to-face setting.

Dourish, Adler, Bellottio and Henderson (1996) report on a similar study in which groups were distributed using GDST and audio-conferencing. The findings indicated that groups using GDST were less satisfied with the meeting process and discussion outcome than non-GDST groups. Also, the study suggested that use of GDST in a distributed environment could have a more negative effect on perceptions of satisfaction than face-to-face use of GDST.

While these studies focused on comparing face-to-face and audio-conferenced settings with and without GDST, not a single study could be found that added a video layer to a distributed meeting to test its impact, with and/or without the use of GDST. The present investigation is meant to start filling this gap by including video-conferencing in the integrated distributed meeting environment being tested. However, integrating group communications and decision support solutions involves several disciplines that contribute to our understanding of human-technology interactions, group processes and dynamics, and group communication (Short, Williams, & Christie,

1976). This is why it has been argued that an interdisciplinary approach is needed for such an evaluation, one that includes engineers, psychologists, social scientists, and linguists. Though daunting, this kind of approach is necessary if we are to understand how media work as integrated environments, how people work in groups and organizations, and how technology affects them all.

Face-to-Face Versus Distributed Meetings

Dourish, Adler, Bellottio and Henderson (1996) stated that: "face-to-face communicative behavior in the real world is not always an appropriate baseline for the evaluation of mediated communication. Moving away from this perspective allows us to explore a number of important, intrinsic properties of video as a communicative medium in its own right."

In today's work environment, meetings are an integral component of the way work gets done. Advances in technology have made it possible for meetings to take place almost anywhere or anytime. This is particularly valuable to organizations seeking to find ways to enable personnel to work together from various locations around the globe. New technologies offer alternatives to face-to-face meetings. However, our understanding of the elements that make distributed meetings successful is much less expansive than that of face-to-face meetings, simply because face-to-face meetings have been around longer, and thus have been more heavily researched. There also may be distinctions between these elements as they apply to small workgroups (3-7 persons) as compared to large task forces or groups (8 and more). In fact, such distinctions are well-documented in group dynamics studies. For this reason, we have chosen to focus on small workgroups.

The Importance of Perception in Distributed Environments

Short et al., (1976) argue that the ways in which people perceive communication media has a lot to do with group and individual social psychology. In this regard, perception is an extremely sensitive element that affects the rate of technology adoption and usage. The authors make the point that communication "media have their own effects and will alter the world in their own ways dependent on their own intrinsic natures."

In general, the study of groups has shown that telecommunications as a way of supporting interaction between group members has an impact on the perception of human relations and social organization. Short et al., (1976) argue that human adjustments to telecommunications solutions might trigger sociological reactions to telecommunications, in turn affecting human adjustments, or lack of adjustments, to them. Should this happen, a distinction between telecommunication solutions that can be provided to meet stated needs and those people would choose to use will become obvious, which will impact which solutions will be used. The point that I want to stress here is that users' perceptions are an important trigger for any technology system usage.

Methods

Participants

The sample was drawn from professionals in a large (2,000 employee) non-profit organization in Washington, DC. Three-hundred thirty-four professional staff members in Washington were invited to participate. One-hundred fifty accepted the invitation, and 72 were randomly selected as participants to reflect the organization's demographics (78% females and 22% males).

Design

A two-factor (GDST vs. No GDST) by two-factor (audio vs. video-conferencing) repeated measures design was employed. Eighteen groups were constructed, with four randomly assigned persons per group. Two groups were assigned to a face-to-face meeting environment as a baseline. Eight groups were randomly assigned to meet using GDST, and eight without GDST. Except for the baseline groups, each group participated in two sessions: one using audio-conferencing (AC) and the other using video-conferencing (VC).

Settings

Two identical conference rooms in the same building were used to simulate the physical setup of a distributed meeting. One room was referred to as the Dallas office and the other as the Atlanta office. The two rooms were identical with regard to furniture, size, color, and lighting. Groups using GDST had laptops in front of each participant and one laptop for the technical facilitator. The laptops were connected to a local area network (LAN) and ran Ventana Corporation's GroupSystems V for Windows™, an electronic meeting system software package.

In the AC setting, subjects were linked by an audio-conferencing facility running on a fiber optics cable. The audio used in the experiment was high-quality, full-duplex and directional for both input and output, which provided almost zero delay. In the VC setting, subjects were in separate meeting rooms but could see each other through a two-way full-duplex high-resolution (30 frames/sec) analogue video-conferencing setup. The setup essentially allowed for direct eye contact between participants, and included a full-duplex audio link.

Monitors were 25" TV monitors, with cameras positioned on top of the TV five feet from participants. Besides manipulation of the two independent variables—using GDST and the communication medium—all other potential sources of variation were either controlled for or randomized.

Sequence of Events

Groups in all treatment conditions followed the same sequence of events, and meetings were videotaped. All participants received an e-mail notifying them about the study date scheduled for their group. A meeting initiator was present in all settings to assist in starting the meeting. The initiator welcomed subjects and then outlined the agenda from a script. At the end of the session, the group had the opportunity to engage in an open discussion regarding the experiment. Group members followed the same process:

1. Subjects were asked to fill out a pre-session questionnaire to provide background information about their prior experiences and exposure to the communication media and GDST, as well as standard demographic data.

2. All groups were asked to follow the same general decision-making steps shown below. This placed some structure on the session, but allowed free-flowing discussion.

- Read case
- Initiate discussion
- Generate ideas
- Select best top-five ideas
- Rank ideas
- Submit list of all generated ideas and the ranked top-five ideas.

3. At the end of each session, group members were asked to fill out a post-session questionnaire. The groups were given a time limit of 40 minutes to complete each session.

For groups using GDST, a technical facilitator was present to help participants use the tools and commands of the GDST as needed. The facilitator was present in one of the two physical conference rooms and was moved to the other room in the second session.

Tasks

DeSanctis & Gallupe, (May 1987) suggested three categories of contingencies for the effect of GDST. The first is communication condition or mode (face-to-face or dispersed), the second is group size (small groups or large groups), and the third is task type. According to McGrath, (1984), task types can be categorized as follows: generate, choose, negotiate, and execute. The task used in the current study required generating ideas, negotiating to categorize the ideas, and choosing the top five ideas. These tasks promoted a goal-based model of collaboration within the allocated time frame.

Two tasks selected to simulate a thinking team engaged in a decision-making meeting were used; each group completed both. The tasks can be classified as Type 4 tasks—decision making tasks with no a *priori* right or wrong answer (McGrath, 1984; Chidambaram & Bostrom, 1993). One task required participants to come up with ideas for improving working conditions; the other focused on ways to compensate and reward teams. All staff members were internally motivated to contribute ideas about improving the working conditions and to explore ways to compensate teams since the individuals participated in multiple teams. The tasks required no specialized knowledge, other than a general business background.

Evaluation Instruments

Dependent variables examined included: a) perception of media, b) perception of meeting quality and c) participants' satisfaction, and performance of the groups. The perception of media dimension was composed of three measures: a) perception of social presence, b) perception of communication effectiveness, and c) perception of communication interface. Two measures were performance indicators: the number of alternatives generated in each meeting, and the time needed by the group to complete the task.

Perception of media was evaluated by a previously validated post-session questionnaire that measured social presence, communications effectiveness, and communications interface (Chidambaram & Jones, 1993).

Perception of quality was measured by a five-question instrument based on the work of Gouran, Brown, & Henry (March 1978), and was measured according to the following: a) confidence with the output, b) agreement with the output, c) impact of the technologies on the meeting effectiveness, d) even participation, and e) overall quality.

Participants' satisfaction was measured by a five-question instrument (Jarvenpaa, Rao, & Huber, 1988) that measured satisfaction with the output, satisfaction with the process, satisfaction with the progress towards the goals of the task, agreement among team members towards the stated goals, and freedom to participate and contribute ideas.

Two measures were used to assess group performance: the number of unique alternatives generated in each session, and the meeting's total duration. The number of alternatives generated was calculated from computer logs, participants' notes, and flip charts. Meeting

duration was determined by calculating the actual time the group needed to complete the tasks and was measured by reviewing the videotapes.

Results

Multivariate Analysis of Variance (MANOVA) was used to identify the combined effects of communication medium (audio-conferencing or video-conferencing) and group decision support tools. The post-hoc analysis was based on the recommendation of Chidambaram & Jones (1993) and Keppel (1982). Whenever a combined difference was observed, follow-up univariate tests were conducted to identify the differences (Chidambaram & Jones, 1993; Huck, Cormier, & Bounds, 1974). Table 1 presents means and standard deviations for all study conditions and dependent variables.

Perception of Communication Media

Hotelling's T^2 multivariate test was used to measure the combined effect of GDST and communication medium on the perception of media by combining the three dependent variables that form the perception of media: social presence, communications effectiveness, and communications interface (Norman & Streiner, 1986). In a synchronous distributed setting, choice of communication medium had an effect on the perception of media, F MANOVA $(3,60) = 8.69$, $p<.001$). VC was the medium that most positively impacted the perception of media. GDST use had no impact on the perception of media. The interaction effect of GDST and communication medium had no effect on the perception of media.

The results of the statistical analysis on each dependent variable composing the perception of media indicated that in a

Table 1

Variables Dependent on Communication Medium: Descriptive Statistics[1]

Group Decision Support Tools (Between Subjects Factor)	Communications Medium (Within Subjects Factor)		Grand Means (Std. Dev.)
	Audio-conferencing	Video-conferencing	
Social Presence			
NO GDST	4.88 (1.06)	5.91 (0.75)	5.40 (1.05)
GDST	5.08 (1.07)	5.40 (0.93)	5.24 (1.01)
Grand Means	4.98 (1.06)	5.65 (0.89)	
Communications Effectiveness			
NO GDST	4.60 (0.97)	5.48 (0.79)	5.04 (0.99)
GDST	4.54 (1.06)	4.96 (0.72)	4.75 (0.93)
Grand Means	4.57 (1.01)	5.22 (0.80)	
Communications Interface			
NO GDST	4.82 (1.13)	5.62 (0.82)	5.22 (1.06)
GDST	4.67 (0.99)	5.07 (1.02)	4.87 (1.02)
Grand Means	4.75 (1.06)	5.34 (0.96)	
Perception of Quality			
NO GDST	5.51 (0.90)	5.84 (0.81)	5.67 (0.86)
GDST	5.21 (1.01)	5.41 (0.96)	5.31 (0.98)
Grand Means	5.36 (0.96)	5.62 (0.91)	
Personal Satisfaction			
NO GDST	5.83 (0.81)	5.99 (0.75)	5.91 (0.78)
GDST	5.26 (1.02)	5.39 (0.82)	5.32 (0.92)
Grand Means	5.54 (0.96)	5.69 (0.84)	

[1]Means are shown with standard deviations in parentheses.

distributed synchronous meeting environment, GDST use did not have an effect on the perception of media. For groups that did not use GDST, VC, as opposed to AC, was the factor that impacted their perception of media. For groups using GDST, no difference between AC and VC was detected.

Social presence. The interaction effect of GDST use and Communications Medium was significant for the social presence measure [F MANOVA $(1, 62) =$ 6.05, $p<.02$]. Collapsing the data on GDST and running the paired samples t-test for all groups using AC and all groups using VC resulted in the perception of higher social presence for VC than for AC [t (63) = 4.49, $p<.001$]. The main effect for Communications Medium is explained by the interaction [F MANOVA $(1,62) = 21.80$, $p<.001$].

Communication effectiveness. The interaction between GDST use and Communications Medium had no effect on the perception of communication effectiveness. The main effect came from Communications Medium [F MANOVA $(1,62) = 23.62$, $p<.001$]. Examination of the means from Table 1 indicates that VC was more effective than AC in communication effectiveness.

Communications interface. The interaction between GDST use and Communications Medium had no effect on the perception of communications interface. Again the main effect came from Communications Medium [F MANOVA $(1,62) = 15.42$, $p<.001$]. Examination of the means from Table 1 indicates that VC was more effective than AC in communications interface.

Perceptions of the quality of the meeting outcome and process. The two dependent variables that compose the perceptions of meeting process and outcome (perception of quality and personal satisfaction) were combined as before. In a synchronous distributed setting, the use of GDST had a negative impact on these perceptions [F MANOVA $(2, 61) =7.51$, $p<.001$]. The communication medium made no difference with regard to the perceptions of meeting process and outcome, and the interaction between GDST use and Communications Medium had no effect on the perceptions of meeting process and outcome.

Perceptions of quality of the meeting outcome. There was a main effect of Communications Medium [F MANOVA $(1,62) = 2.26, p<.04$]. Examination of the means from Table 1 indicates that VC meetings were perceived as having higher quality than AC meetings. An item analysis confirmed this same pattern for the three questions comprising perceived meeting quality. There was no main effect for GDST use or the interaction between GDST use and Communications Medium.

Participants' personal satisfaction. There was a main effect for GDST use [F MANOVA $(1,62) = 7.14$, $p<.01$]. Examination of the means from Table 1 indicates that non-GDST meetings were perceived as more satisfying than GDST meetings. An item analysis confirmed this same pattern for the five questions comprising satisfaction. There was no main effect for Communications Medium or the interaction between GDST use and Communications Medium.

Performance of Groups

A repeated-measures MANOVA was conducted to test the combined effect of GDST use and Communication Medium on the performance measures. Means and standard deviations are presented in Table 2.

There was no evidence to indicate that GDST increased the number of alter-

Table 2

Audio and Video Performance Measures: Descriptive Statistics[1]

Group Decision Support Tools (Between Subjects Factor)	Communications Medium (Within Subjects Factor)		Grand Means (Std. Dev.)
	Audio-conferencing	Video-conferencing	
Number of Alternatives Generated			
NO GDST	20.00	18.75	19.38
	(4.24)	(12.51)	(9.05)
GDST	23.75	24.50	24.13
	(7.382)	(9.636)	(8.30)
Grand Means	21.88	21.63	
	(6.13)	(11.19)	
Meeting Duration			
NO GDST	36.38	35.16	35.77
	(7.23)	(6.55)	(6.69)
GDST	40.19	39.19	39.69
	(7.87)	(6.72)	(7.08)
Grand Means	38.28	37.17	
	(7.56)	(6.74)	

[1]Means are shown with standard deviations in parentheses.

natives generated by the groups. The meeting time was 40 minutes for each session, and groups were reminded of the remaining time twice throughout the session. While there seems to be a tendency for the second meeting to take less time than the first, the results of the analysis did not indicate any difference among the groups.

Discussion

Perception of Communication Media

Three measures comprised the perception of media: perception of social presence, perception of communication effectiveness, and perception of communication interface. The results indicated that, when no GDST were used, VC had an impact on the perception of communication media, while AC did not. When GDST were used to support the meeting, there was no evidence that GDST had an impact on the perception of media, and it did not matter whether AC or VC was used to support the meeting.

One practical implication of this finding is that organizations can capitalize on the benefits of using GDST in distributed meeting environments without losing much in terms of the perceptions of communication media. If organizations decide to use GDST, VC appears not to add much to the perception of media; AC appears to be sufficient. When GDST are not available, VC makes the difference in terms of perceptions of communication media.

Social Presence

It was thought that VC would positively impact perceptions of social presence. This hypothesis was supported only for groups that did not use GDST alone. This in itself is a finding worth elaborating on, since it has a implications for business. VC made all the difference when compared to AC alone. However, when GDST were introduced, it did not make any difference whether VC or AC was used. In reviewing the videotapes, it was found that 50 to 60 percent of the meeting duration was allocated by the groups for brainstorming and idea-generation. The rest of the time was used for ranking, voting, and finalizing the decision. During the idea generation phase, groups using GDST hardly used the conferencing media, so it did not matter whether VC or AC was available. Without GDST, the groups felt that VC provides a much broader social bandwidth, since it allows them to receive non-verbal communication cues. Such cues are very important (Stevens & Finlay, 1996; Zigurs, Poole, & DeSanctis, December 1988), since many of the rules that set the boundaries of interpersonal relationships in organizations are implied by nonverbal communication (Baskin & Aronoff, 1980; Stevens & Finlay, 1996). This finding is actually consistent with those of several studies that compare AC with VC (Yoo, 1996).

The groups did not differ on the social presence measure. The expectations were that GDST would minimize the perception of social presence. This conclusion is actually consistent with the work of Chidambaram & Jones (1993), in which they compared AC and face-to-face meetings with and without the use of GDST and found that the use of GDST in an AC session did not decrease perception of social presence, although in face-to-face meetings it did. Thus, the finding that

GDST use decreases perceptions of social presence in face-to-face meetings was not replicated in distributed meetings.

The reason for such findings could be that participants perceive the distributed environment as simply different from face-to-face interaction in terms of being less social. The addition of GDST did not really decrease or affect that perception. Also, recall the suggested meeting process that the groups followed. This process did not promote the use of GDST as the means to come up with the final decision. The groups had the freedom to use the tools if they so wished. At the same time, use of GDST was balanced with discussion around the ideas generated, classification of ideas, and agreement on the final list. The availability of the conferencing media allowed group members to ask each other questions in order to clarify an idea that they read on the screen. So GDST was not a limiting factor in this regard.

Another way to consider this finding is that GDST may promote anonymity, and anonymity does not promote social closeness. While the degree of anonymity is thought to have a major impact on group perceptions, processes and outcome (Jessup, Connolly, & Galegher, September 1990; Nunamaker, Applegate, & Konsynski, 1988; Stevens & Finlay, 1996), it did not seem to be an issue for the group members here. This could be attributed to the small size of the group, or to the fact that the power and status relationships between and within groups were relatively equal, since all participants were within the same professional and management levels within the organization.

Communication Effectiveness

As for the impact of the communication media on communication effectiveness, it was found that VC increased perceptions of effectiveness when no GDST were used. This is not surprising, since VC establishes a much richer communication channel and thus is perceived as a more effective communication medium when compared with AC only. When GDST were not used, it was clear that VC helped in reducing uncertainty and increasing communication effectiveness. In some of the sessions where GDST were not used, participants utilized the video channel to write the ideas on a flip chart, to raise a piece of paper in front of the camera, or simply to sense each other's comfort level with the ideas being discussed. Video allowed participants in both locations to work together as one team and to reduce the group/location effect by keeping everyone engaged.

The business implication of this finding is that participants using GDST in a distributed setting can maintain effective communication simply by using AC. The cost of adding VC does not buy the organization much in terms of perceived communication effectiveness. If no GDST are used, VC will almost definitely add to the perception of communication effectiveness.

Improving communication effectiveness has to do with reducing uncertainty and resolving equivocality (Chidambaram & Jones, 1993). Our hypothesis that GDST would increase perceptions of effectiveness was not supported. This result was not expected and certainly contradicts other research findings (Chidambaram & Jones, 1993). However, the limited experience the groups had with using VC and GDST may help to explain this finding. The use of VC may have been so fascinating and so enjoyable that introducing GDST did not serve to increase the participants' perceived effectiveness.

Communication Interface

The communication interface findings are consistent with social presence and communication effectiveness, and the same interpretations apply here. The business implication of such findings is that organizations can get all the benefits of using GDST in distributed meetings without losing much in terms of perceptions of communication interface. If GDST are used, AC will be sufficient. Adding VC increases cost with little or no benefit if GDST are used. Without GDST, video enhances the interface.

Communication interface refers to the actions required of participants in order to activate a communication session and exchange information. It was hypothesized that the more actions were required, the lower the perception of communication interface would be. Hence, when GDST were used, it was expected that the perceptions of communication interface would decrease. This was not supported. The other hypothesis, that VC will enhance perception of communication interface, was supported for groups not using GDST.

Perceptions of the Quality of the Meeting Outcome and Process

The general findings are that VC contributed positively to the perceived quality of the meeting output and process. This conclusion supports the finding of Olson, et al. (Olson & Olson, 1997; Olson et al., 1997) that in distributed synchronous meetings with no video connection, the participants reported that the quality of the discussion was significantly poorer. When participants used audio only, they reported that the communication medium gets in the way of convincing the other side of the merit of their ideas. The perception of the participants is that the video clearly adds value. These findings conflict with earlier research that video does not add real value to meetings.

There was no evidence that GDST use enhanced the perceived quality. On the contrary, GDST use decreased the participants' satisfaction with the meeting.

Perception of Quality

The perceived quality of both the meeting process and the outcome benefited from the use of VC. This is mainly due to the fact that video enhances the users' experience, helps in interpreting the visual information communicated, increases awareness, and establishes identity and recognition, especially when participants have never seen each other before. Video seems to make people feel willing to communicate with each other.

GDST, however, was not perceived as enhancing the quality of the meeting. This finding was definitely not expected, but it could be attributed to the lack of group experience with using such tools to structure meetings. Since 60 percent of the participants reported that they had previously seen or used GDST in a face-to-face meeting, their prior experience might have had an impact on their perception. It would be interesting to reassess the groups' reaction to the use of GDST after an extended period of frequent use.

Participants' Personal Satisfaction

In general, there was no evidence that VC enhanced personal satisfaction. The use of GDST clearly decreased satisfaction. This could be attributed to the unnaturalness and unfamiliarity of the setting as compared to that of face-to-face meetings, which the group members are more used to. It should be recognized that to the participants this was a new working environment, and that may have had an unsettling effect.

Performance of Groups

The two elements used as performance quality measures were the number of alternatives generated in the meeting and the duration of the meeting. The data indicate that the number of alternatives generated when groups used GDST was higher than when groups did not use GDST, but this trend was not significant. Also, meeting time increased when participants used GDST, but again this trend was not significant. In general, the second session that each group conducted took less time and generated more alternatives, regardless of the communication media used or whether GDST were used. This could be due to the fact that the group's experience in the first session with the use of the technology and the suggested meeting process then shortened the learning curve in the second session, as was usually observed.

Number of Alternatives

The use of GDST in a distributed environment did not increase the number of alternatives generated, although there was a trend in that direction. Also, the use of VC did not seem to make a difference in the number of ideas generated in the meeting. However, considering the direction of the data, there is an indication that groups using GDST and VC generated more ideas than any other groups. At the same time, groups using VC only generated fewer ideas than other groups. This observation suggests the need to investigate this issue with further research, since we were not able to detect evidence of the impact of the setting on the number of alternatives generated.

Meeting Duration

Groups that met using only VC took the shortest time to complete the task. However, these groups also generated the lowest number of alternatives. This finding also calls for more investigation, since it raises the question of whether VC by itself distracts the group from focusing on the issue and completing the task.

Comparing face-to-face meetings with distributed meetings, however, is not likely to give us the useful distinctions we need to advance our understanding of these types of meetings. Rather, we need to compare different types of distributed meetings, using different combinations of technologies, with one another to produce a truer picture of the variations within the dynamics of dispersed teamwork—including the factors that determine success and the barriers that impede it. Because of the technologies involved in these types of meetings, our approach to studying them should draw on research on emergent communicative practices rather than looking to transfer our knowledge of face-to-face meetings to dispersed environments. By focusing on how these technologies—namely AC and VC, with or without augmentation by GDST—affect individual perceptions of and satisfaction with meeting outcomes, we can better gauge how group decision-making and interaction are aided or impaired when communication cannot take place face to face. In short, the present study is grounded in the assumption that face-to-face and technologically aided dispersed meetings are fundamentally different types of social interactions and communication environments. These findings, I believe, demonstrate that the approach taken here will prove a more fruitful path for researchers to follow in future studies.

Conclusions and Implications for Further Research

The use of GDST in a distributed same-time environment did not decrease the perceptions of social presence or communication interface. At the same time, GDST did not increase perceptions of communication effectiveness or quality. However, GDST use decreased individual personal satisfaction with the meeting.

We found that when groups are meeting without the use of GDST, VC was perceived as a significant element that increased perceptions of social presence, communication effectiveness, communication interface, and perception of quality. However, the use of video did not enhance individual personal satisfaction with the meeting. Conversely, when groups met using GDST, there was no detected difference between AC and VC in terms of perceptions of social presence, communication effectiveness, communication interface, quality, and personal satisfaction.

Regarding the number of alternatives generated and the meeting duration, no difference was detected between AC and VC, with and without GDST. However, trends in the data indicate that the tendency of groups using GDST was to generate more ideas in the meeting and to require more time to complete the task than groups not using GDST. This trend needs to be explored with further research. No difference was detected between groups in terms of the quality measures as they relate to the use of audio-conferencing or video-conferencing.

Although considerable research has been conducted on the dynamics of face-to-face meetings and on comparisons of face-to-face meetings with meetings using AC, we cannot yet claim to fully understand all the dynamics involved in every type of group meeting environment. Since today's mobile and global business culture makes distributed meetings virtually a necessity, the need to better understand the elements that make for successful distributed meetings is great.

It is worth noting that the findings from this research, though they can have value for the design of any integrated solution to support distributed synchronous work, are situational and therefore only applicable to the parameters and variables described. The meta-variables that exist in any group meeting study are numerous and interrelated. A change in a meta-variable might lead to a different conclusion, should the conditions of this study be altered. In addition, this study was conducted in a non-profit organization where the general culture values providing better services. Such an environment, though it may strive to encourage efficiency, focuses more on effectiveness. This cultural bias could be an important variable in participants' satisfaction; thus, it would be interesting to replicate this study in a for-profit organization.

References

Anderson, A. H., O'Malley, C., Doherty-Sneddon, G., Langton, S., Newlands, A., Mullin, J., Fleming, A. M., & Van der Veldon, J. (1997). The impact of VMC on collaborative problem solving: An analysis of task performance, communicative process, and user satisfaction. In K. E. Finn, A. J. Sellen, & S. B. Wilbur (Eds.), *Video-mediated communication* (pp. 133-155). Mahwah, NJ: Lawrence Erlbaum Associates, Inc., Publishers.

Baskin, O. W., & Aronoff, C. E. (1980). *Interpersonal communication in organizations*. Santa Monica, CA: Goodyear Publishing Co.

Boland, R. P., Maheshwarl, A. K., Te'eni, D., Schwartz, D. G., & Tenaski, R. V. (1992, October 31-November 4). *Sharing perspectives in distributed decision making*. Paper presented at the Computer Supported Cooperative Work CSCW'92, Toronto, Canada.

Buckley, S. R., & Yen, D. (1990). Group decision support systems: Concerns for success. *The Information Society, 7*, 109-123.

Cass, K., Heintz, T. J., & Kaiser, K. M. (1992). An investigation of satisfaction when using a voice-synchronous GDSS in dispersed meetings. *Information & Management, 23*, 173-182.

Chapanis, A., Ochsman, R. N., Parrish, R. B., & Weeks, G. D. (1972). Studies in interactive communication: The effects of four communication modes on the behavior of teams during cooperative problem-solving. *Human Factors, 14*, 487-509.

Chidambaram, L., & Bostrom, R. P. (1993). Evolution of group performance over time: A repeated measures study of GDSS effects. *Journal of Organizational Computing, 3*, 443-469.

Chidambaram, L., & Jones, B. (1993). Impact of communications medium and computer support on group perceptions and performance: A comparison of face-to-face and dispersed meetings. *MIS Quarterly—Management Information Systems, 17*, 465-491.

Dennis, A. R., George, J. F., Jessup, L. M., Nunamaker, J. F., Jr., & Vogel, D. R. (1988). Information technology to support electronic meeting. *MIS Quarterly, 12*, 591-624.

DeSanctis, G. L., & Gallupe, R. B. (May 1987). A foundation for the study of group decision support systems. *Management Science, 33*, 589-609.

Di Pietro, C. (1995). Meetingware and organizational effectiveness. In D. Coleman & R. Khanna (Eds.), *Groupware: technology and applications* (pp. 437-472). Englewood Cliffs, NJ: Prentice-Hall.

Dourish, P., Adler, A., Bellottio, V., & Henderson, A. (1996). Your place or mine? Learning from long-term use of audio-video communication. *Computer Supported Cooperative Work: The Journal of Collaborative Computing, 5,* 33-62.

Dykstra-Erickson, E., Rudman, C., Marshall, C., Hertz, R., Mithal, K., & Schmidt, J. (March, 1995). *Supporting adaptation to multimedia desktop conferencing.* Paper presented at the International Conference on Human Factors in Telecommunications, Melbourne, Australia.

Finn, K. E. (1997). Introduction: An overview of video-mediated communication literature. In K. E. Finn, A. J. Sellen, & S. B. Wilbur (Eds.), *Video-mediated communication* (pp. 3-22). Mahwah, NJ: Lawrence Erlbaum Associates, Inc., Publishers.

Fish, R. S., Kraut, R. E., & Chalfonte, B. L. (1990). *The VideoWindow system in informal communication.* Paper presented at the Proceedings of the Computer-Supported Cooperative Work —'90, New York.

Fish, R. S., Kraut, R. E., Root, R. W., & Rice, R. E. (1992). *Evaluating video as a technology for informal communications.* Paper presented at the CHI'92 Conference Proceedings, New York.

Gaver, W., Smets, G., & Overbeeke, K. (1995). *A Virtual window on media space.* Paper presented at the ACM Conference on Human Factors in Computing Systems, CHI'95 Conference Proceedings, New York.

Gouran, D. S., Brown, C., & Henry, D. R. (March 1978). Behavioral correlates of perceptions of quality in decision-making discussions. *Communication Monographs, 45,* 51-63.

Gray, P., Vogel, D., & Beauclair, R. (1990). Assessing GDSS Empirical Research. *European Journal of Operational Research, 46,* 162-176.

Harmon, J., Schneer, J. A., & Hoffman, R. L. (February 1995). Electronic meetings and established decision groups: Audioconferencing effects on performance and structural stability. *Organizational Behaviour and Human Decision Processes, 61,* 138-147.

Harrison, S. (1992). *Making a place in media space* (Technical Report SSL-92-42). Palo Alto, California: Xerox Palo Alto Research Center.

Heath, C., & Luff, P. (1992). Media space and communicative asymmetries: Preliminary observations of video-mediated interaction. *Human-Computer Interaction, 7,* 315-346.

Huck, S. W., Cormier, W. H., & Bounds, W. G., Jr. (1974). *Reading statistics and research.* New York, NY: Harper & Row.

Isaacs, E. A., & Tang, J. C. (1993). *What video can do and can't do for video collaboration: A case study.* Paper presented at the ACM Multimedia 93, New York.

Jarvenpaa, S. L., Rao, V. S., & Huber, G. P. (1988). Computer support for meetings of groups working on unstructured problems: A field experiment. *MIS Quarterly, 12,* 645-666.

Jessup, L. M., Connolly, T., & Galegher, J. (September 1990). The effects of anonymity on GDSS group process with an idea-generating task. *MIS Quarterly,* 313-321.

Johansen, R., Martin, A., Mittman, R., Saffo, P. I., Gibbet, D., & Benson, S. (1991). *Leading business teams.* Addison-Wesley.

Lucas, H. J. (1981). *Implementation: The*

key to successful information systems. New York: Colombia University Press.

Maaranen, P. (1995). *GroupVideo— Distributed EMS for small groups.* Paper presented at the Proceedings of the 28th Annual Hawaii International Conference on System Sciences, Hawaii.

McGrath, J. E. (1984). *Groups: Interaction and performance.* Dee Amir Josephson (Ed.). Englewood Cliffs: Prentice Hall.

Norman, G. R., & Streiner, D. L. (1986). *PDQ statistics.* Toronto: B.C. Decker, Inc.

Nour, M. A., & Yen, D. C.-C. (1992). Group decision support systems: Towards a conceptual foundation. *Information and Management, 23,* 55-64.

Nunamaker, J., Vogel, D., Heminger, A., & Martz, B. (June 1989). Experiences at IBM with group support systems: A field study. *Decision Support Systems, 5,* 183-196.

Nunamaker, J. F., Applegate, L. M., & Konsynski, B. (1988). Computer-aided deliberation: Model management and group decisions support. *Journal of Operational Research, 6,* 826-848.

Nunamaker, J. F., Briggs, R. O., & Romano, N. C. (1995a). *Meeting environments of the future: Meeting to plan work or meeting to do work?* (pp. 20). Publisher on the Word Wide Web at www.ventana.com/library/ Future.pdf.

Nunamaker, J. F., Dennis, A. R., Valacich, J. S., Vogel, D. R., & George, J. F. (1991). *Electronic meetings to support group work. communications of the ACM, 34,* 40-61.

O'Conaill, B., Whittaker, S., & Wilbur, S. (1993). Conversation over video con-ferences: An evaluation of the spoken aspects of video-mediated communi-cation. *Human-Computer Interaction, 8,* 389-428.

Olson, G. M., & Olson, J. S. (1997). Making sense of the findings: Common vocabulary leads to the synthesis necessary for theory building. In K. E. Finn, A. J. Sellen, & S. B. Wilbur (Eds.), *Video-mediated communication* (pp. 75-91). Mahwah, NJ: Lawrence Erlbaum Associates, Inc., Publishers.

Olson, J. S., Olson, G. M., & Meader, D. (1997). Face-to-face group work compared to remote group work with and without video. In K. E. Finn, A. J. Sellen, & S. B. Wilbur (Eds.), *Video-mediated communication* (pp. 157-172). Mahwah, NJ: Lawrence Erlbaum Associates, Inc., Publishers.

Olson, J. S., Olson, G. M., & Meader, D. K. (1995). *What mix of video and audio is useful for small groups doing remote real-time design work?* Paper presented at the CHI'95 Conference Proceedings, New York.

Pagani, D. S., & Mackay, W. E. (1993). *Bringing media spaces into the real world.* Paper presented at the Proceedings of ECSCW'93, Milan.

Pinsonneault, A., & Kraemer, K. (1990). The effects of electronic meetings on group processes and outcomes: An assessment of the empirical research. *European Journal of Operations Research, 46,* 143-161.

Rutter, R. R., Stephanson, G. M., & Dewey, M. E. (1981). Visual com-munication and the content and style of conversation. *British Journal of Social Psychology, 20,* 41-52.

Sellen, A. J. (1995). Remote conversa-tions: The effects of mediating talk with technology. *Human-Computer Interaction, 10,* 401-444.

Short, J., Williams, E., & Christie, B. (1976). *The social psychology of telecommunications.* John Wiley & Sons.

Stevens, C. A., & Finlay, P. N. (1996). A research framework for group support systems. *Group Decision and Negotiations, 5,* 221-243.

Tang, J. C., & Issacs, E. (1992). *Why do users like video? Studies of multimedia supported collaboration* (TR-92-5). Mountainview, CA: Sun Microsystems Laboratories.

Turoff, M., Hiltz, S. R., Bahgat, A. N. F., & Rana, A. R. (1993). Distributed group support systems. *MIS Quarterly,* 399-417.

Watson, R. G. (1987). *A study of group decision support system use in three and four person groups for a preference allocation decision.* Unpublished doctoral dissertation, University of Minnesota.

Yoo, Y. (1996). *The effects of group development on the utilization of video channel and decision quality of distributed decision making groups.* Paper presented at the the Second Americas Conference of the Association for Information Systems, Phoenix, AZ.

Zigurs, I., Poole, M. S., & DeSanctis, G. L. (December 1988). A study of influence in computer-mediated group decision making. *MIS Quarterly, 12,* 625-644.

[2]*Correspondence to:*
Tony F. Habash, D.Sc.
Information Technology Services Group, AARP
601 E Street, N.W.
Washington, D.C.
E-mail: thabash@aarp.org

[3]The views presented here are those of the author and do not necessarily represent the policies or viewpoints of AARP.

---

[1]Tony F. Habash, D.Sc. This article is based on a dissertation submitted to the George Washington University in partial fulfillment of requirements for a Doctorate of Science degree.

Section IV:

THE LAST PAGE

The Psychologist-Manager Journal
1999, Vol. 3, No. 2, 233-234

The "Practice" of Management

Rodney L. Lowman[1]
California School of Professional Psychology

David Mamet (2000) noted that "The purpose of literature is to Delight." The purpose of management, I contend, is somewhat less singular. It is both to help create vision, purpose, and wonder and — sometimes simultaneously, sometimes not — to create and maintain control. On the one hand, the manager tries to help create things that, but for his or her managerial expertise, would otherwise not happen, but also to execute control over actions and people, events, and circumstances that too often exist in a state of disarray.

The "practice" of management implies two things. First, as practitioners of a profession, managers, and especially psychologist-managers, aim to apply what is already known to the problems of management. When confronted with a new managerial concern, psychologist-managers do not create a response by intuition or hunch, or by starting from scratch, but rather scour the literature and apply the theory and empirical research of both psychology and management, and of psychology-management, to these issues.

The practice of the profession of psychology-management requires the integration of psychology to management. This requires deriving practice from theory and from empirical research about what works and what does not. The practice benefits from familiarity with, and reliance upon, an emerging and ever-accreting literature, access to which is the *sine qua non* of thoughtful management.

For psychologist-managers to read the studies and writings of management, they must of course first know that they exist. Psychologist-managers taking their craft seriously must be able to access quickly the "psychology-management" literature in the relevant archival databases, such as psychology's *PsycINFO*. Knowledge of that literature base is what differentiates the professional psychologist-manager from the intuitive one.

As a new journal, *The Psychologist-Manager Journal* aims to contribute to that knowledge, research and practice base. Unfortunately, traditionalists, such as those apparently contributing to decisions about including the journal in relevant databases, do not always understand the research and theory base of management, nor may they understand the theory- and data-driven nature of psychology-management. A recent decision, currently under appeal, for example, by the American Psychological Association not to archive the contents of this journal in the *PsycINFO* database illustrates the distance between the academic enterprise, at least as it is sometimes practiced, and the psychologist-managerial agenda. A letter from the APA boldly, if inelegantly, asserted: "[sic] *Psychologist-Manager Journal* has been evaluated by the staff of *PsycINFO* according to its policy guidelines for accepting relevant journals...Our evaluation proved to show [sic] that the articles are not research or theory based analyses nor of archival quality. The articles serve to be [sic] largely up-to-the-minutes [sic] advice verses [sic] academic/theoretical based research."

Prejudice against psychology-management as a discipline, if that is what such decisions reflect, is not new. Perhaps as much as musicians and actors, who, as creative talents, are similarly dependent on, and ambivalent toward, their leaders, gatekeepers of the academic enterprise seem not to admire management or to take it seriously as an application worthy of study in its own right. Yet management is the glue that allows the vested interests of academics, among many others, to achieve their individual and collective goals. Imagine orchestras without leaders, plays without directors, universities without presidents. Imagine further managers and leaders without knowledge, who do not take their craft or their profession seriously enough to read or understand or practice its literature base.

The "practice" of psychology-management can also be taken in a second way. We rarely get things right the first time around, particularly when learning to conduct ourselves in areas for which we are untrained and for which we do not consult the literature. The practice of management suggests not only that it is a profession that is anchored in a literature base, but that we have an obligation to keep trying to get it a little closer to right. As John Irving put it in a book from which I quoted in the first issue of this journal: "I have never thought of myself as a 'born' writer—any more than I think of myself as a 'natural' athlete, or even a good one. What I am is a good rewriter; I never get anything right the first time— I just know how to revise, and revise" (Irving, 1996, p. 127).

References

Irving, J. (1996). *Trying to save Piggy Sneed.* New York: Arcade Publishing.

Mamet, D. (2000, January 17). Writers on writing. The humble genre novel, sometimes full of genius. New York *Times*, Internet: *www.nytimes.com/library/books/011700mamet-writing.html.*

[1]*Correspondence to:*
Rodney L. Lowman, Ph.D.
System Dean's Office
College of Organizational Studies
California School of Professional Psychology
6160 Cornerstone Court East
San Diego, CA 92121
E-mail: rlowman@cspp.edu

For Product Safety Concerns and Information please contact our EU representative GPSR@taylorandfrancis.com Taylor & Francis Verlag GmbH, Kaufingerstraße 24, 80331 München, Germany

T - #0189 - 270225 - C0 - 254/178/6 - PB - 9780805894776 - Gloss Lamination